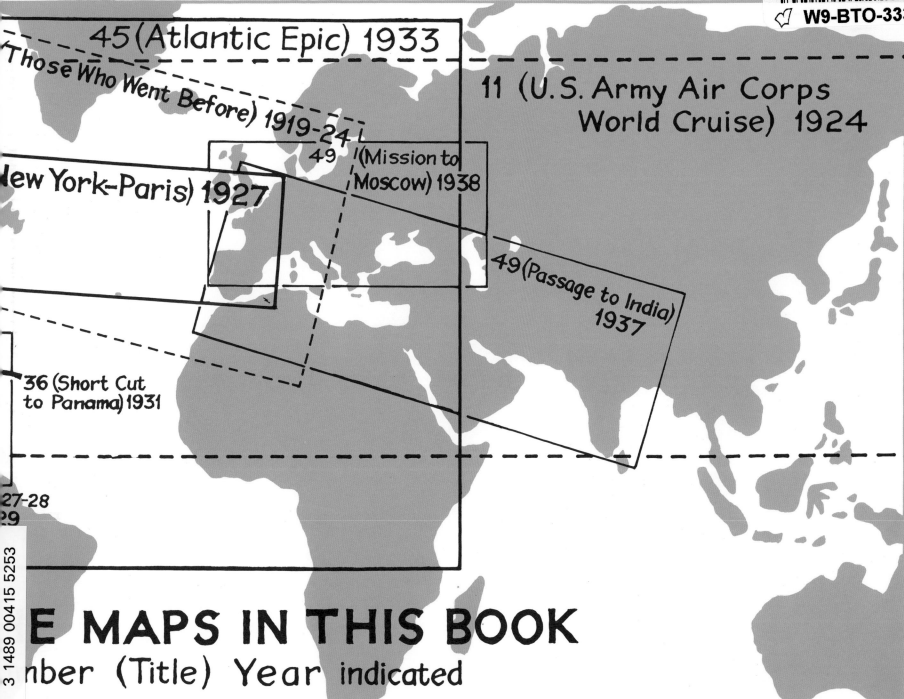

45 (Atlantic Epic) 1933

(Those Who Went Before) 1919-24

11 (U.S. Army Air Corps
World Cruise) 1924

(New York-Paris) 1927

49 (Mission to
Moscow) 1938

49 (Passage to India)
1937

36 (Short Cut
to Panama) 1931

27-28
29

E MAPS IN THIS BOOK

mber (Title) Year indicated

CHARLES
LINDBERGH

AN AIRMAN, HIS AIRCRAFT, AND HIS GREAT FLIGHTS

OTHER BOOKS BY R.E.G. DAVIES

A History of the World's Airlines
Airlines of the United States Since 1914
Airlines of Latin America Since 1919
Continental Airlines—The First Fifty Years
Rebels and Reformers of the Airways
Pan Am: An Airline and Its Aircraft
Lufthansa: An Airline and Its Aircraft
Delta: An Airline and Its Aircraft
Aeroflot: An Airline and Its Aircraft
Fallacies and Fantasies of Air Transport History
Commuter Airlines of the United States
(with Imre Quastler)
Saudia: An Airline and Its Aircraft
TransBrasil: An Airline and Its Aircraft
Airlines of Asia Since 1920

CHARLES
LINDBERGH

AN AIRMAN, HIS AIRCRAFT, AND HIS GREAT FLIGHTS

by R.E.G. Davies
Illustrated by Mike Machat

Paladwr Press

Published by Paladwr Press, 1906 Wilson Lane, #101, McLean, Virginia 22102-1957, USA

Manufactured in Hong Kong

Book Design by R.E.G. Davies

Artwork by Mike Machat

Maps by R.E.G. Davies

Technical editing by John Wegg

Typesetting/Layout by Spot Color, Oakton, Virginia

Prepress and press management by The Drawing Board

ISBN 1-888962-04-6

First Edition

Contents

Foreword by Dr. Tom Crouch

At precisely 5:52 on the afternoon of July 2, 1939, Charles Augustus Lindbergh lifted an Army P-36A off a runway at Denver, Colorado, and headed westwards toward Salt Lake City. He had returned to America from an extended stay in Europe on April 14. Four days later he had accepted General Henry H. "Hap" Arnold's invitation to go on active duty as a Colonel in the Army Air Corps. Since that time, his military duties, and his consulting work for the National Advisory Committee for Aeronautics and the Guggenheim and Rockefeller Foundations, had kept him constantly on the move, and in the air.

Over the past two and one half months he had made two flights from a field near his home on Long Island to Dayton, and had made round trip solo flights to Buffalo, Indianapolis, and Kansas City. Between May 1 and May 13, he made a solo, coast-to-coast flight with stops in Dayton; St. Louis; Marshall, Kansas; Albuquerque; Winslow, Arizona; March Field, California; San Diego; Los Angeles; Tucson; Roswell, New Mexico; Midland, Texas; and Charlotte, North Carolina.

Climbing away from the Denver airport on that July afternoon, Lindbergh was setting out on the sixth leg of yet another transcontinental solo flight. He had a great deal on his mind. At each stop he had encountered "the usual press nuisance." Newsmen had been an inescapable and unwelcome presence in his life since he had soloed across the Atlantic in May, 1927. Angered by the constant harassment of reporters and photographers during the long months of horror following the kidnapping and murder of his son in 1932, he had moved his family to Europe late in 1935, not long before the execution of Richard Bruno Hauptmann for the crime.

Since his return to the U.S., however, he had begun to make use of the press to publicize his opinions on the international situation. He had seen German military might at first hand, and was impressed. Convinced that sinister foreign influences would attempt to draw the United States into any future conflict with the fascist powers, Lindbergh was increasingly determined to do what he could to maintain American neutrality. It would not, he knew, be an easy fight.

As always, however, he left those problems behind him as he climbed into the sky. "The high peaks are so close to Denver," he would report in his diary that evening, "that I had to climb the plane almost at its maximum rate to get over them without circling."

I climbed . . . and rode on top like a god —the cloud-strewn sky, the white-capped peaks, the rain-filled valleys, mine. I owned the world that hour I rode over it, cutting through my sky, laughing proudly down on my mountains, so small, so beautiful, so formidable, I could dive at a peak; I could touch a cloud; I could climb far above them all.

Born almost two years before the Wright brothers' epoch-making flight, Charles Lindbergh was the most celebrated aviator of the 20th century, and one of the most controversial figures of his generation. Just as Americans would never forget the incredible wave of enthusiasm and pride that washed across the nation in the wake of his flight from New York to Paris in May 1927, neither would many of them forgive him for the attitudes and opinions that he expressed during the months and weeks before Pearl Harbor.

As R.E.G. Davies reminds us, however, Lindbergh was the consummate aviator, whatever his political attitudes. The book that you hold in your hands focuses on the great flights that made newspaper headlines and shaped the growth and development of aviation during the years between the wars. It reminds us that Lindbergh was unquestionably the most experienced pilot of his day. Those weeks in the spring of 1939 when he was repeatedly winging from coast-to-coast were typical for him at the peak of his career. It is difficult to imagine that anyone logged more hours in the air than Charles Lindbergh did during the years 1925–1940.

And if no one spent more time in the air, few individuals described their experience more eloquently than Charles and Anne Morrow Lindbergh. Ron Davies has provided a fine introduction to their great flights, setting them in the larger context of aviation history. I urge everyone who is fascinated by the story told in this book, however, to treat themselves to the poetry of *The Spirit of St. Louis*, *Of Flight and Life*, *Listen, the Wind!*, *North to the Orient*, or any one of the other books in which these two consummate author/aviators described their journeys through life, as well as through the air. You will not be disappointed.

In 1927, this young man, 25 years old—he seemed little more than a teenager—posed for a cameraman at Roosevelt Field, Long Island, New York, on 20 May 1927.

Acknowledgements
Unless otherwise indicated, all photographs in this book have been selected from the extensive collection at the National Air and Space Museum of the Smithsonian Institution. I also thank the Charles A. Lindbergh House of the Minnesota Historical Society, at Little Falls; the C.R. Smith Museum of American Airlines at Dallas; David Ostrowski of *Skyways* magazine; Fred Roos, of the Missouri Historical Society. John Wegg, of *Airways* magazine.

Hugh Cowin, Dennis Wrynn, J.M. Mitchelhill, and Sam Smith provided previously unpublished photographs. Daniel P. Kusrow kindly lent the rare Lindbergh flight cover on page 26. Virginia Barnes and Robin Sterling prepared the index. Artist Mike Machat and graphic designer Jennifer Sterling offered good suggestions, while Sam Smith, John Wegg, and Jackie Scott-Mandeville provided the essential copy-editing and proof-reading necessary to maintain Paladwr Press's high standards of presentation and accuracy.

Introduction

Author's Preface

The name Charles Lindbergh was almost omni-present in every facet of the development of aviation during the span of his flying life. He started as a young man, eager to fly; sought aerial adventure as one of the early barnstormers; did a spell with the Air Corps; and by 1926 was the chief pilot of one of the very first airlines—one of the ancestors of today's American Airlines. In the following year he attained instant celebrity status by flying from New York to Paris, solo, nonstop.

Such was the world acclaim of this achievement—a genuine case of fact being more incredible than fiction—that the event transcended almost everything else he subsequently did in the furtherance of aviation knowledge and experience. More books have been written about Lindbergh than of any other famous aviator, even including Antoine St Exupéry, who is close to sanctity in the eyes of most Frenchmen. And about half the content of these books concentrates on the great flight of the *Spirit of St. Louis* on 20/21 May 1927.

Undoubtedly, this had been an adventure of legendary proportions. But Lindbergh historians have not recognized his other work with the same determination and fervour that he had applied to winning the Orteig Prize. True, the tragic episode of the death of his first son has been recounted, often in great detail, almost like a detective story. The unfortunate distraction and curiously misled diversion into the field of international politics, and his irresponsible affair with the America First isolationist movement that preceded the United States's entry into the Second World War: these subjects have been well covered. But insufficient attention has been given to all the effort that Charles Lindbergh made in popularizing aviation in the eyes of all Americans, including the political leaders, business tycoons, and the ordinary man-in-the-street.

This book attempts to redress some of the neglect and to emphasize that Lindbergh's flying career embraced invaluable survey and planning work for two pioneering airlines, Pan American Airways and T.W.A. He demonstrated that crossing the oceans with load-carrying aircraft was not the apparently insuperable dream that was held, even by advanced aviation authorities, in the early 1930s. His circumnavigation of the Atlantic Ocean in 1933 was a masterpiece: but its reporting was obscured, or at least diluted, by his estrangement from his own country in the latter 1930s, as he fled from press harrassment. And his unpopularity with the Roosevelt administration tended to prolong his disappearance from the public eye, except for non-aviation involvement—for which he had only himself to blame.

These pages concentrate on the neglected aspects of a great aviation career, and focus on those episodes that have received scant recognition in the past: his work in popularizing aviation with goodwill tours, planning the transcontinental air route for T.W.A., and above all, the so-called *Jelling* expedition that took him and his wife on their trans-Atlantic odyssey in 1933. Some readers may discover interesting additions to Lindbergh folklore.

This book is primarily about Charles Lindbergh's role as an aviator, not forgetting the substantial contribution made by his wife, Anne, co-pilot, navigator, radio operator, and faithful diarist. On the other hand, mention has to be made about his political digressions, as they were too emphatic to be ignored. Equally, full credit is given to his wartime aviation years, in which he made valuable contributions to the techniques of aircraft production, specification, and performance. By these efforts, he went a long way towards redeeming himself from the shame of his America First involvement and his apparent sympathies with Nazi Germany.

The author and artist-collaborator hope that this book will be a useful addition to the vast library of literature on the life of a great man. Whatever his shortcomings in some directions, he had no equal as a superb pilot and intuitive navigator who, during the 1930s, did more than any other individual to create airmindedness in the United States. This became a national preoccupation, and one that was to lead to American dominance of an entire world industry.

R.E.G. Davies

Artist's Note

I was honored to have this opportunity to pay artistic tribute to one of the greatest names in aviation history. As a 'post-World-War II' specialist, I usually focus much of my attention to the supersonic world of flight test, the development of jet-age commercial aviation, and aircraft of the modern era. What a rare treat, however, to delve into the exotic 'Golden Age' from the exciting period between the World Wars, when barnstorming, flying the mail, and trailblazing new commercial airline routes were the cutting edge of aerial technology.

Like the great classic automobiles of this era, airplanes personified their builders, and names like Curtiss, Ryan, de Havilland, and Sikorsky came to symbolize a never-to-be-repeated romantic age in aviation. As an artist, I gained a new appreciation for the complex structure of the early biplanes, the myriad color schemes of the mailplanes and barnstormers, and the flowing art-deco lines of the seaplanes and flying boats. As a pilot, I gained a tremendous respect for the accomplishments of this great aerial pioneer who conquered incredible navigational obstacles without the aid of radar, Loran, or ground controlled approaches, and who successfully flew to the four corners of the globe without the assistance and pinpoint accuracy of global positioning satellites.

This commentary would not be complete without mention of Machat's Law, which deals with the constant inconsistencies of aircraft color schemes and configurations. In innumerable cases where material simply did not exist regarding a *specific* aircraft flown by Charles Lindbergh, I have chosen to illustrate the best example of that particular type of airplane, such as the World War II fighters. Where information allowed, I have depicted an *exact* aircraft flown by Lindbergh, such as the obvious one-of-a-kind Ryan 'NYP,' the colorful modified Lockheed Sirius, and the last of four de Havilland DH-4 mailplanes operated by Robertson Aircraft Corporation.

As with all previous Paladwr Press books I have had the pleasure to illustrate, there is a vast support network lurking behind the scenes to assist with the intense research effort that is so critical to ensure the accuracy and detail that have become the hallmark of Ron Davies's works, and I would like to extend my personal thanks to these individuals without whose assistance this artwork simply would not have been possible. Aviation historian and meticulous aircraft restorer Tom Crowder unearthed innumerable Lindbergh treasures from his vast aviation library at Santa Paula, California, mecca for Golden Age aviation, and the works of fellow-Santa Paula resident and renowned artist Walt 'Matt' Jefferies, creator of so many wonderful profiles, three-views and cutaways of these magical aircraft, yielded a treasure trove of information. Aviation artist Craig Kodera generously assisted with the initial stages of fact-finding, and Mr. George Rutledge offered many insights into the Robertson Air Mail chapter. (Upon my questioning the DH-4's colors, he commented that he knew they were accurate because he was the one who painted those very aircraft). Special thanks also to Jay Miller and Frank Strnad. I hope you share the excitement that Ron and I both experienced in creating this wonderful book.

Mike Machat

Growing Up

The Parents

Charles Augustus Lindbergh, Jr., was born on 4 February, 1902, the son of a politician of the same name, of Swedish immigrant ancestry. Lindbergh Senior first married Mary LaFond in 1887, and had three daughters; but Mary died in 1898, aged only 31, and he was married again, on 27 March 1901, to Evangeline Land. They lived in Little Falls, Minnesota, although young Charles was born in Detroit.

Charles, Senior, became a Congressman for the 6th District of Minnesota in 1907, won the seat again in 1914, albeit by a lower margin; and then ran as a Senatorial candidate but lost in the primaries. Later, in 1918, he also ran for the state governorship, but lost again. These losses were during the period of the Great War of 1914–18, and the elder Lindbergh was not only against U.S. intervention in that war, but was also anti-Catholic, both of which persuasions no doubt weighed against him. Two decades later, his son was to carry on the isolationist tradition, with similar effect on his popularity.

The Home

The younger Charles grew up in a Huckleberry Finn environment at Little Falls, on the banks of the upper reaches of the Mississippi. When still young, he was a good woodsman, an excellent marksman, and an ingenious do-it-yourself improviser. He was a hardy youth—he slept on the porch, even in severe weather. And he was mechanically-minded— he drove his father's Model T Ford at the age of 12 during the 1914 election campaign. Two years later, he was driving a Saxon Six.

During his early years he was not well educated in the academic sense, preferring to spend more time farming, but he did attend Wisconsin University when he was 18. Then after two years, on 22 March 1922, he dropped out, as he had decided to become an airplane pilot. He went to Lincoln, Nebraska, on 1 April, and learned to fly at the Nebraska Aircraft Company. On 9 April, with Bud Gurney (who was later to become a close friend) he took his first flight in a Lincoln Standard.

Having developed a strong physique and an enduring stamina during his early youth, and having taken his first flying lessons in his early twenties, Charles Lindbergh was ready to embark on a flying career.

Young Charles, as a boy, pictured with his mother.

Charles Lindbergh, the young man.

Like most children, Charles loved animals, and is pictured here with his friend, Dingo.

The young Charles Lindbergh, with his father, Charles Senior.

The Barnstormer, 1922–23

Curtiss JN-4 Jenny

Length/Span:	.27/44 feet
Engine	Curtiss OX-5 (90 hp)
Seating	.2 (inc. pilot)
Cruise Speed	.60 mph
MGTOW	.2,000 lb
Normal Range	.200 st. miles

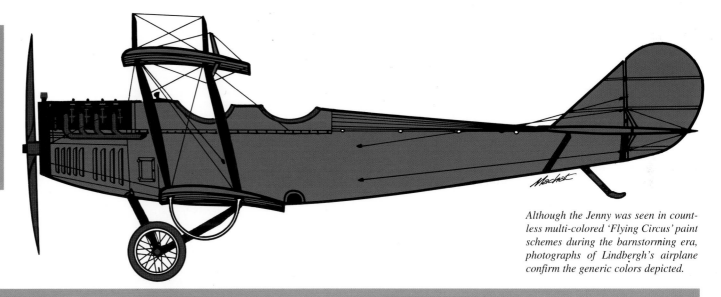

Although the Jenny was seen in countless multi-colored 'Flying Circus' paint schemes during the barnstorming era, photographs of Lindbergh's airplane confirm the generic colors depicted.

Barnstorming

In these years, the United States public regarded airplanes as risky, even dangerous, contrivances, and classified the intrepid aviators (and occasional aviatrixes) rather in the same category as death-defying trapeze artists. Individual airmen, or groups of them, would tour the countryside, like travelling circuses, and they became known as barnstormers.

Young Lindbergh, fresh from having just made his first flights, joined up with Erold Bahl, one such barnstormer, and in May and June 1922 toured Nebraska, Kansas, and Colorado. He was nothing if not adventurous, indeed almost fearless. He did the then fashionable 'wing-walking,' learned to parachute-jump from Charlie and Kathryn Hardin, and progressed to the risky 'double-jump' performance. Late in June, with H.J. Lynch, Banty Rogers, and Booster the dog, he barnstormed in the northern Prairie States, in a Lincoln-Standard biplane, achieving local fame as 'Daredevil Lindbergh.' By the late summer of 1922, he had gone as far as Billings, Montana, and returned to Lincoln in October by canoe and boat.

In April 1923, he bought a Curtiss Jenny for $900.00, barnstormed again from Mississippi to Minnesota, wrecked the aircraft on 8 June 1923, flew in Leon Klink's Canuck (Canadian-built Jenny), and campaigned for his father in between more barnstorming. He took his mother on a flight, met up with Bud Gurney again, and sold the repaired Jenny.

Early in 1924, another flying colleague, Marvin Northrop, gave him the idea of joining the Army, and his way of life changed, although his inclination towards taking risks did not.

Charles Lindbergh went barnstorming in 1922 and 1923, visiting more than a dozen states in the mid-west, the south, and the prairies.

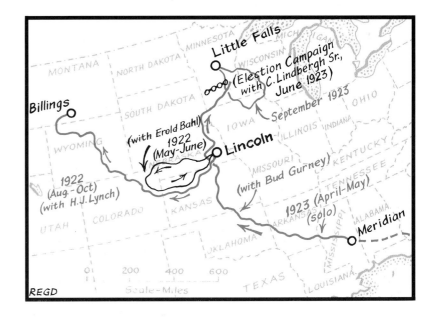

Those Who Went Before

Lt. Cdr. A.C. Read (right) and some of his crew (plus a naval man) of the NC-4.

British pilots John Alcock and Arthur Whitten-Brown.

Major G.H. Scott, Commander of the rigid airship, R34.

Leigh Wade, of the Douglas World Cruisers expedition.

Dr. Hugo Eckener, German promoter of airships, delivered the LZ126 (ZR3).

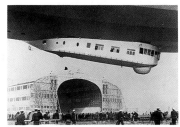

The Curtiss NC-4, first aircraft to reach Europe, at Lisbon

The Vickers Vimy World War I bomber, which crash-landed in Ireland.

The British airship made the round trip, without much incident.

World Cruiser No. 4 New Orleans *seen here refuelling.*

The spacious LZ126 gondola contrasted with the cramped airplane cockpits.

America Lags Behind

Sporadic activities such as barnstorming and fixed-base operations for charter work and flying schools seemed to be the limit of vision of those concerned with aviation in the United States, at least until the mid-1920s. Meanwhile, in other parts of the world, elementary forms of government-sponsored or supported air transport were forging ahead, in Latin America and Australia, Asia, and Africa, and especially in Europe. By 1926, almost every country in Europe, even diminutive Albania, had infant air route systems; and the leading countries each boasted several airlines. In the U.S.A. entrepreneurial attempts had, in direct contrast, been short-lived, the most successful, Aeromarine, lasting only from 1920 to 1923.

The Atlantic Conquered

Many believe that Charles Lindbergh was the first man to fly across the Atlantic. His great achievements were threefold: (1) he made the first solo flight; (2) he made the journey non-stop between the two continental land-masses, not between off-shore islands; and (3) he landed exactly where he aimed to go. But no less than 117 individual flights had been made across the Atlantic before May 1927, some by the shorter South Atlantic crossing, a few via the island-hopping northern perimeter. Of the 105 who flew across the North Atlantic, including the World Cruisers (see page 12) 62 had been in the British airship R34, flying in both directions, and one of these, westbound, was a stowaway.

The perceived hazards of the journey discouraged further attempts, until the second announcement of the Orteig Prize in 1926 (see page 16).

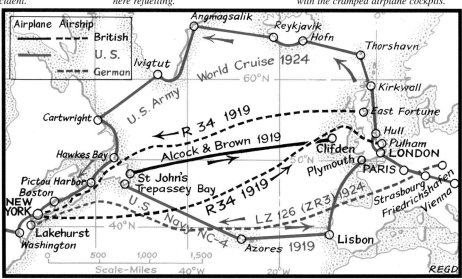

This map shows the routes of the 105 individual crossings of the North Atlantic before Charles Lindbergh's.

The Pathfinders of 1924

The Unprecedented Air Journey

One of the surprising facts in aviation history lies in the paradox that one of the greatest pioneering achievements attracted far less than its fair share of recognition as such. For in 1924, four Douglas aircraft set off from California on a U.S. Army Air Corps mission whose target was no less than to accomplish a circumnavigation of the world. The route, which officially started at Seattle, had to avoid over-water journeys of more than about 700 miles, simply because the aircraft, even specially equipped, did not have the range. Therefore, the itinerary headed northwest to Alaska, across northeastern Siberia, through Japan and Southeast Asia, across the Indian subcontinent, the Middle East, Europe, Iceland, Greenland, and finally back across North America. The ambitious exercise was breathtaking in its scope.

The Douglas World Cruisers

Of the four aircraft that took off from Seattle on 6 April 1924, the *Seattle* did not go very far. It crashed in Alaska, and dropped out of the round-the-world attempt. The other three, the *New Orleans*, the *Boston,* and the *Chicago*, by a combination of determined perseverance and military discipline, all managed to reach Iceland. Bearing in mind that sometimes the floats (pontoons) had to be exchanged with the wheels, and the load of both types of gear carried throughout (sometimes by supply ships), this was a truly admirable accomplishment, and evidence of the quality of both the crew and the aircraft.

Boston was lost, while flying between the Shetland Islands and Iceland, but another World Cruiser, also named the *Boston,* set off from Santa Monica to meet the two survivors, and the trio arrived back triumphantly at Seattle on 28 September.

The Example

This was during the era when aviators world-wide were seeking fame, certainly, and perhaps fortune, by making flights that beat records of some kind, either for speed, or height, or distance. The World Cruisers did none of these, but they forged a route pattern, indeed several of them. Their objective was to reach a destination, and to do this, they were not averse to using convenient setpping-stones, close to the 'Great Circle' routes, which offered shorter itineraries than the apparently direct lines on some map projections. Within a decade, Charles Lindbergh and his wife were to follow in their wake.

The Douglas World Cruiser Seattle *is pictured here at anchor at Kanatak, Alaska.*

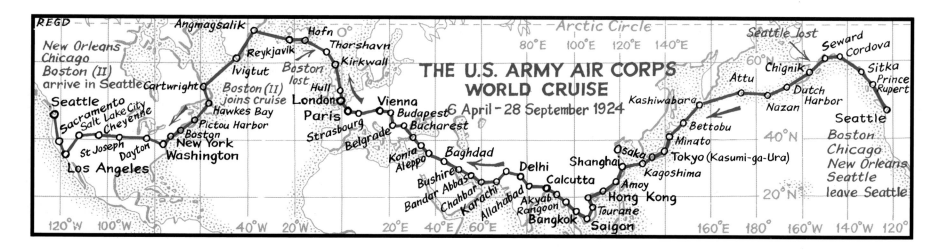

The National Guardsman, 1924

Lincoln Standard

Length/Span: . . . . .27/44 feet
Engine . . . . .1 Hispano-
Suiza (150 hp)
Seating . . . . .3, inc. pilot
Cruise Speed . . . . .85 mph
MGTOW . . . . .2,200 lb
Normal Range . . . . .200 st. miles

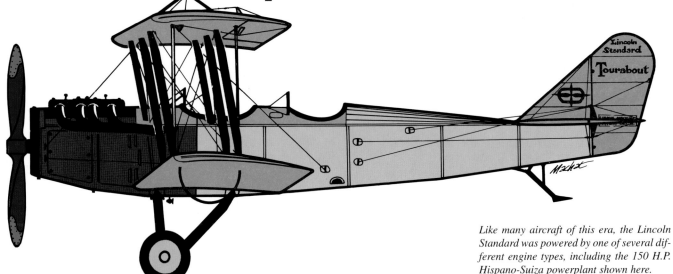

Like many aircraft of this era, the Lincoln Standard was powered by one of several different engine types, including the 150 H.P. Hispano-Suiza powerplant shown here.

The Cadet

On 9 March 1924, Charles Lindbergh reported for examinations as a flying cadet with the Missouri National Guard. Four days later he was in the Army, for a one-year stint. Those twelve months were quite eventful. He was regularly top of the class, and in spite of a dramatic crash on 6 March 1925, when he had to take to his parachute from his Royal Aircraft Factory S.E.5a during a simulated dog-fight with a de Havilland, he qualified as a pilot on 16 March.

Caterpillar Club

He returned to St. Louis on 25 March, did some more barnstorming with Wray Vaughan, and made his second lifesaving parachute-jump on 2 June 1925, thus qualifying himself as a card-carrying member of the Caterpillar Club. Most of his flying was done in a Lincoln Standard biplane.

Charles Meets the Robertsons

Back in St. Louis by October 1925, he met war veterans Bill and Frank Robertson, who had established a flying school with sundry charter or contract work. He was offered a job and once again, Charles Lindbergh's way of life changed.

Charles Lindbergh and his friend Bud Gurney.

The young cadet in the U.S. Army Air Service Reserve at Kelly Field, Texas, in March 1925.

Flying the Mail, 1926

De Havilland (Dayton Wright) DH-4B

Length/Span:	.31/42 feet
Engine	Liberty 12A (400 hp)
Seating	.1 pilot
Cruise Speed	.105 mph
MGTOW	.4,600 lb
Normal Range	.400 st. miles

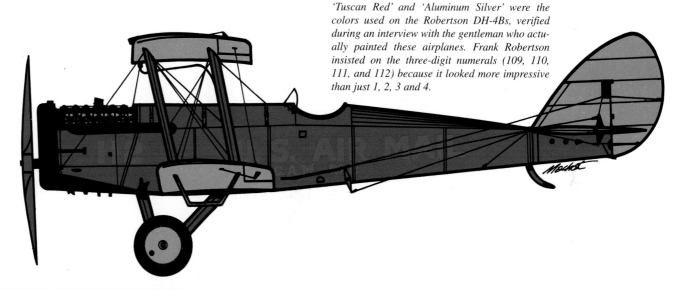

'Tuscan Red' and 'Aluminum Silver' were the colors used on the Robertson DH-4Bs, verified during an interview with the gentleman who actually painted these airplanes. Frank Robertson insisted on the three-digit numerals (109, 110, 111, and 112) because it looked more impressive than just 1, 2, 3 and 4.

May Carry Mail to Chicago

SAVES LIFE

FLYER DROPS MILE TO SAFETY IN FOG

C. A. Lindbergh, Mail Aviator, Plunges 5000 Feet to Earth Successfully With Parachute When Clouds Prevent His Landing in Plane—Drops in Cornfeild Uninjured and Finds Wrecked Ship.

CHICAGO, Sept. 17.—The story of Carl A. Lindbergh, the air mail pilot who saved his life in a parachute when his plane ran out of gasoline, 4,000 feet over Ottowa, Ill., is chief pilot for the St. Louis-Chicago air mail route. He piloted the first plane of this route, April 15, when the service was inaugurated. He is considered one of the best fliers in the air mail service.

C. A. LINDBERGH.

These newspaper extracts illustrate the infancy of the contract air mail services in the United States, and also provide a glimpse of Charles Lindbergh's involvement. The picture of the DH-4B mailplane on the left was printed at the time of the 'Kelly' Act of 1925; the center picture shows Charles Lindbergh, the chief pilot of Robertson Aircraft Corporation, delivering the first sacks of mail to St. Louis from Chicago on 15 April 1926; while the extract and picture on the right, dated 17 September, is a reminder of the hazards of flying the mail in those days. (Courtesy: C.R. Smith Museum, American Airlines.)

The Mail Man

The Kelly Act

On 2 February 1925, the United States Congress passed the Air Mail Act, the so-called 'Kelly Bill,' named after the sponsoring representative. Since 1919, the U.S. Post Office had pioneered the carriage of mail by air, and had built up both an impressive nationwide network of routes and a good record of service. Now, the burgeoning volume of traffic had created a situation in which the Post Office's air transport organization was (it had more than 200 aircraft) becoming too big to manage. The Kelly Act authorized the piecemeal transfer of the air mail routes to private operators under the familiar process of awarding contracts to the lowest bidder. On 15 April 1926, the Robertsons inaugurated C.A.M. (Contract Air Mail) Route No. 2 to carry the United States mail between Chicago and St. Louis.

Flying the Mail

Charles opened the Robertson Air Corporation's Chicago–St. Louis mail contract service, flying a DH-4B over the route, with stops at Springfield and Peoria. True to form, he managed to derive some adventure from this ostensibly routine operation. He made his third life-saving parachute jump at Ottowa airfield, Chicago, on 6 September (see page 13), and his fourth, at Cowell, Illinois, on 3 November of that year. During his period with Robertson he also managed to do some stunting in St. Louis, as well as to indulge in his habit of playing practical jokes on his co-pilots. But on one occasion, they returned the compliment. After a deep sleep one night, the result of a typically long and hard day's flying, he woke up in the morning, still in his bunk-type bed, to find himself very much alone in the middle of the airfield.

Chief Pilot

By this time, Charles Lindbergh had earned a reputation as a skilled pilot, and a daring one. In the mid-1920s, this latter characteristic was not considered to be a deficiency, quite the opposite. Such was the reliability (or lack thereof) of the aircraft of the 1920s, and such was the inaccuracy of flying instruments (a simple compass and unreliable altimeter were typically the total aids to navigation) that all pilots had to be daring, as a pre-requisite. The Robertsons (see page 10) offered Charles the position as chief pilot, presiding over a fleet of ten de Havilland DH-4Bs (plus four more as standbys) and two Curtiss Orioles.

Charles Lindbergh standing in front of a Curtiss Robin with Bill Robertson, president of the Robertson Aircraft Corporation.

ROBERTSON AIRCRAFT CORP.
1926

CHICAGO
Yorkville
La Salle
Joliet
Morse

Peoria
Pekin
Mason City

Springfield

Carlinville

ST. LOUIS

Emergency fields

Mississippi River

ILLINOIS

Missouri R.

0   50   100   150
Scale - Miles

REGD

The quintessential air mail pilot. Charles Lindbergh, Chief Pilot of the Robertson Aircraft Corporation, poses with one of the mail carrier's Douglas M-4s.

The Experience

With his responsibility as the Robertsons' chief pilot, Charles Lindbergh's application to the methods of regular air operations went into a new learning stage. He had been given full authority to plan the entire CAM route, controlling not only the aircraft fleet, but also to organize the local surface installation requirements of the nine landing fields (including emergency strips) that were needed for the operation. Such a combined application of careful planning, strict discipline, and shrewd judgement was to serve him well, as no other form of academic or other training could have done, in the months to come.

Ready for take-off while flying on the Contract Air Mail Route No. 2 (C.R. Smith Museum). The aircraft was a Pitcairn Mailwing.

After his second parachute jump with the Robertsons, Charles's only injury was a sprained wrist.

Charles Lindbergh clutches the historic first sack of mail as he arrived at St. Louis on the Robertson Aircraft Corporation's Chicago–St. Louis air mail route on 15 April 1926. (C.R. Smith Museum)

(Below) This picture captures the essence of a typical scene at an airfield during the embryo years of the contract air mail service. The location is the Robertson Aircraft Corporation's field at St. Louis, probably in 1926. The group of buildings was hardly bigger than a large farm. People wandered into the area without restriction, and took a close interest in the aircraft, even 'inspecting' them. The entire atmosphere was one of casual informality. (C.R. Smith Museum)

The Incentive

The Orteig Prize

Attending a movie theater on 16 September 1926, Charles Lindbergh saw a newsreel item, portraying the Sikorsky S-35, a large tri-motored biplane, that was to be flown by the renowned French aviator, René Fonck, in pursuit of the $25,000 prize offered by a New York restaurateur, Raymond Orteig, to the first pilot to fly non-stop between New York and Paris. Lindbergh was intrigued, possibly because of his own self-confidence, possibly because the prize was worth a small fortune—about $250,000 or more in today's monetary value.

Four days later, when Fonck crashed the S-35 on take-off, he was more than intrigued. Charles was stimulated to carry his keen love of adventure to the impossible dream of entering the competition for the Orteig prize.

The dapper René Fonck, credited with 75 victories as a French ace of World War I, had crashed his tri-motor ignominiously, on 20 September 1926.

The man whose idea started it all: Raymond Orteig, French restaurateur, in happy mood, seen here with his wife while crossing the Atlantic by ship.

During the preparations for the New York-Paris flight, the chief contestants were photographed together. Richard Byrd is in the center, Clarence Chamberlin on the right.

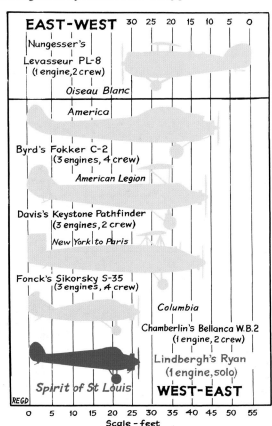

EAST-WEST   30 25 20 15 10 5 0

Nungesser's
Levasseur PL-8
(1 engine, 2 crew)

Oiseau Blanc

America

Byrd's Fokker C-2
(3 engines, 4 crew)

American Legion

Davis's Keystone Pathfinder
(3 engines, 2 crew)

New York to Paris

Fonck's Sikorsky S-35
(3 engines, 4 crew)

Columbia

Chamberlin's Bellanca W.B.2
(1 engine, 2 crew)

Lindbergh's Ryan
(1 engine, solo)

Spirit of St Louis   WEST-EAST

REGD

0 5 10 15 20 25 30 35 40 45 50 55
Scale - feet

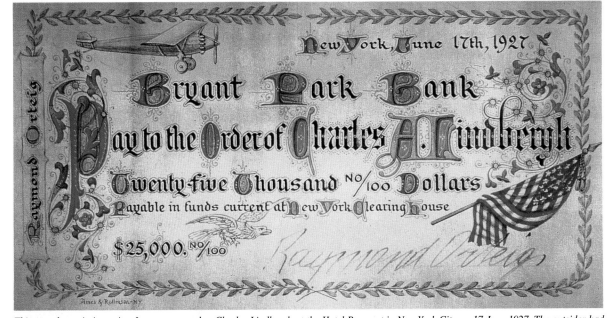

This was the main incentive. It was presented to Charles Lindbergh at the Hotel Brevoort in New York City on 17 June 1927. The outsider had won, handsomely. As the chart at the left shows, the other contenders for the Orteig prize were either multi-crew, or flew multi-engined aircraft, or both. Lindbergh was the only solo, single-engined entrant.

The *Spirit of St. Louis*

This airplane has been photographed at many different stages of its career, but this illustration captures the factory-fresh Spirit *as it appeared when it rolled out at San Diego. The original spinner shown on the aircraft developed a crack during the first cross-country flight, and was replaced with the conical one shown here at Curtiss Field in New York before Lindbergh flew off to Paris. The lettering on the original tires spelled out "Silvertown Airplane Cord."*

Ryan NYP   *("NYP" = New York–Paris)*

Length/Span: ....28/46 feet
Engine ....Wright Whirlwind J-5C (223 hp)
Seating ....1 pilot
Cruise Speed ....105 mph
MGTOW ....5,250 lb

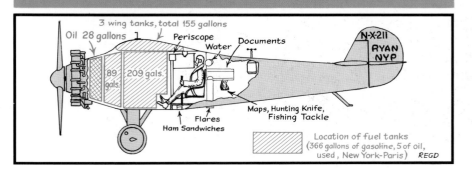

The Choice

He studied the merits of the tri-motored S-35 (and of the twin-engined S-37 replacement) against those of a single-engined aircraft, and decided that the latter's fuel capacity for the 3,600-mile journey outweighed the risk of a catastrophic engine failure in mid-ocean.

After careful consideration, he chose a single-engined model, familiarly known as the Brougham, and built by the Ryan company of San Diego. He made arrangements to have it specially modified, mainly by replacing the passenger accommodation space in the forward section of the fuselage by a large fuel tank. This had the effect of completely obliterating his view (Lindbergh's Ryan had no windshield) and he had to fly by using a periscope mounted on his left side, and occasionally by opening the door on his right.

Back to St Louis

Charles had already gone to San Diego, and under the supervision of Ryan's Donald Hall and Franklin Mahoney, the *Spirit of St. Louis* was prepared for its first flight, which was made without incident on 28 April 1927. Charles Lindbergh spent much of his time at San Diego, keeping a watchful eye on the creation of his special Brougham variant. On hand, incidentally, was Douglas Corrigan, a pilot who was later to make his own extraordinary mark in the annals of Atlantic flight.

Contracting for the airplane, entering the competition, and meeting the expenses: all this had needed financial sponsorship, which had been forthcoming from a group of investors and supporters from St. Louis: Earl Thompson, Major Albert Lambert, Major William Robertson, Harry Knight, Harold Bixby, and others. On 28 February 1927, the formal entry form was completed, and the airplane christened, very appropriately.

Prelude to a Mission

Bad Omens

The portents for flying directly (as opposed to making stops en route) across the North Atlantic Ocean were not good. No crossing had been made by a heavier-than-air machine (as opposed to a rigid airship) since 1924 (see page 11) and this was via the northern perimeter of the Atlantic, stopping at Iceland, Greenland, and other points, where long-range flying capability was not essential. Just after the *Spirit's* first flight, the two Frenchmen, Nungesser and Coli, set off from Paris, but they disappeared without trace in a westbound attempt on 8 May 1927. Had they succeeded, all of Lindbergh's preparations would have been in vain. And, as previously mentioned, René Fonck's preparations also resulted in tragedy (page 16), and the opportunity was still alive.

Good Practice Run

Even if Charles Lindbergh was aware of this event, he was undeterred. On 10–12 May, he flew from San Diego to New York, stopping only at St. Louis, and breaking the transcontinental record in the process. No doubt he also made good use of the time in adapting his flying skills to the new type, and also making a number of mental calibrations that were to serve him well on the great endeavour.

He had made the preparations: to finance the endeavor, to construct the aircraft, to test its performance, and to plan the route, all with great care and attention to detail. Throughout this preparatory period, he appears to have retained a serene equanimity—especially considering the apparent strength of the competition—that belied his years.

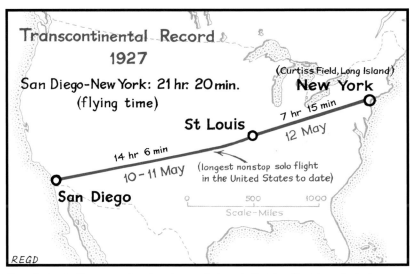

Transferring the Ryan monoplane from its manufacturer to the take-off point required a transcontinental flight. Lindbergh did this with considerable flair, beating the transcontinental speed record, and paying a courtesy visit to his sponsors in St. Louis.

A happy young pilot is photographed with his pride and joy, a specially-modified Ryan Brougham monoplane, at Dutch Flats, San Diego, early in May 1927.

Now christened, the Spirit of St. Louis *takes off from San Diego on 10 May 1927 (at 3:55 p.m.) en route to New York, during its first real test of range and fuel consumption.*

The Great Flight, 1927

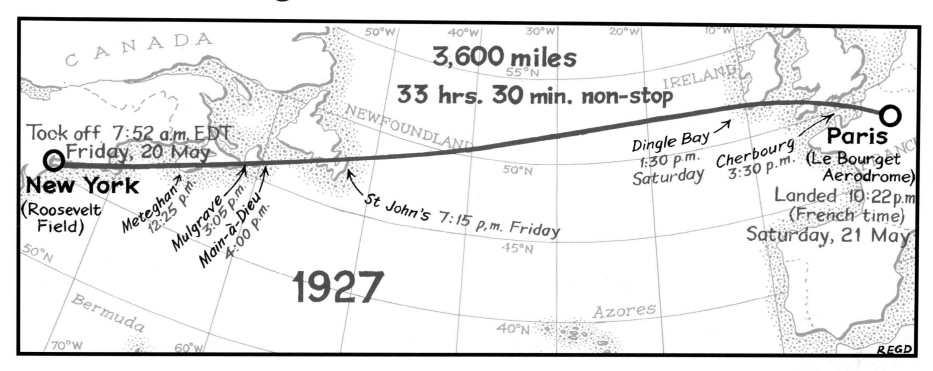

3,600 miles
33 hrs. 30 min. non-stop

Took off 7:52 a.m. EDT
Friday, 20 May
New York
(Roosevelt
Field)

Meteghan 12:25 p.m.
Mulgrave 3:05 p.m.
Main-à-Dieu 4:00 p.m.

St John's 7:15 p.m. Friday

Dingle Bay
1:30 p.m.
Saturday

Cherbourg
3:30 p.m.

Paris
(Le Bourget
Aerodrome)
Landed 10:22 p.m.
(French time)
Saturday, 21 May

1927

The Great Flight

At Roosevelt Field, on Long Island, the poor weather was quite a deterrent. But Charles Lindbergh could be described as a living anti-deterrent. He loved challenges and seemed to thrive on them. He had defied death several times already, and this was, to him, simply a dangerous mission, fraught with risks. But these latter were of a calculated kind, and he had done the calculations. He had mapped out his itinerary, and this was exactly what he set out to do.

Keeping It Simple

To put this flight in perspective, there were more than twenty attempts to fly across the Atlantic in 1927. Several aircraft crashed or made emergency landings, some pilots were never seen again, and only three aircraft—Lindbergh's, Chamberlin's, and Byrd's—actually made it across as a direct result of the Orteig Prize. And as the diagram on page 16 emphasizes, Charles's instinct to 'keep it simple' was intuitively correct. All the other contestants for the Orteig Prize used either multi-engined aircraft, or had 2, 3, or 4-man crews. But the single-engined, solo contestant won.

This picture clearly portrays
Charles Lindbergh's youth—a mere 25 years.

Departure

Take-off

At 7:52 a.m. on 20 May 1927, Charles Lindbergh took off into the morning mists, only just clearing the various obstructions at the end of the field. He made a slight detour from the direct Great Circle route, to St John's, Newfoundland, and then headed east. Equipped with only basic instruments plus a periscope, and fortified by only a couple of sandwiches, his superb navigational prowess brought him across to sight land at Valentia Island, at the entrance to Dingle Bay, in southeastern Ireland, only a few miles off his planned check point.

This was in itself an achievement. All the previous flyers had set off with the objective only to reach land—any land—on the other side of the ocean. Lindbergh's navigation, on the other hand, by day and by night, was precise. Later calculations were to show that his incredible flight deviated from the geographical distance—the Great Circle route—by only 15 miles.

Truth is Sometimes Better than Fiction

Many books have been written about this epic flight. The subject is a good example of when a factual account can capture the imagination better than any work of fiction. The story ended with a young, relatively unknown, young man winning through against all the odds against him: his youth (and therefore presumed inexperience), the strength of the competition, and the considerable demands that would be made on both his physical and mental stamina. His early years at Little Falls had hardened him well against the natural elements; and his air mail experience had led him to an unorthodox balance of consciousness against sleep. During the flight, he stayed awake for 33.5 hours—and this after having had little, if any sleep the night before.

This was the rather austere instrument panel of the Spirit of St. Louis. *The cruise control chart on the right was added after the trans-Atlantic flight.*

Charles Lindbergh poses with the Spirit of St. Louis, *at Roosevelt Field, Long Island.*

On a cold and misty morning, on 20 May 1927, Charles Lindbergh climbs into his flying suit. He took it off about 35 hours later—in Paris.

Arrival

Although heavy with sleep, Lindbergh's adrenalin must have been flowing by the time he crossed southwest England across Cornwall, then the French coast at Cherbourg, to come in to land at Paris's Le Bourget airport at 10.21 p.m. on 21 May 1927, to be greeted by a wildly excited crowd of Parisians whose sheer numbers threatened to endanger the possibility of landing the *Spirit* at all.

The flight had taken 33 hours 30 minutes, which is a long time to stay awake, by any measure. And this was also after hardly a wink of sleep before departure. To remain completely alert for every minute of that time is quite remarkable. But Charles Lindbergh was a remarkable man. He had become the first person to fly alone across the Atlantic Ocean, moreover nonstop between the main land-masses, not between off-shore islands, of both continents. And he had done so at the relatively tender age of 25.

This historic picture shows the crowd scene at Le Bourget Aerodrome in Paris when, at 10:21 p.m. in the late evening, Charles Lindbergh landed as prescribed by Raymond Orteig. The rapturous acclaim of this great achievement is illustrated by a typical newspaper headline and commentary below.

EXTRA ★ **St. Paul Daily News** ★ **SPORTS** COMPLETE N.Y. STOCKS

VOL. XII   THREE CENTS   SATURDAY, MAY 21, 1927   THREE CENTS   NO. 173

LINDBERGH IS IN PARIS

FLIER COMPLETES AIR

Flight Sends Wright Stock Up 5 Points

Instant Hero

During the early 1920s, France had taken the lead in aviation, and was justly proud of its leadership. But young Charles Lindbergh captured the hearts of the French, who fully appreciated both the achievement and the romance of the remarkable flight to Paris. He was immediately honored with the medal of the Légion d'Honneur, and is pictured here with French President Gaston Doumergue (center) and U.S. Ambassador Myron Herrick (right).

The young hero is acclaimed as he leaves the Elyssé Palace (residence of French Presidents, wearing his Légion d'Honneur medal. Ambassador Herrick is on his left.

Inspiration to an Industry

To state that the flight of 'The Lone Eagle' (as he was soon portrayed, by general acclaim) was epoch-making is no exaggeration. This single event altered the entire approach to aviation in the United States, by the public as a whole; by the politicians—who had hitherto been apathetic to aeronautical matters; by the press, which could not find headline type large enough to match its enthusiastic embrace of such a news story; but most of all by the industrialists and investors who lubricated the wheels of American commerce. This young man, hardly beyond college age, had demonstrated that flying was no longer a matter of performing stunts. It had practical possibilities. For the infant airline industry, recently given the basic infrastructure of a regulatory foundation by the 'Kelly' Air Mail Act of 1925 and the Air Commerce Act of 1926, this dramatic aeronautical achievement of 1927 was just the spark that was needed to ignite into flame the smouldering, almost dead, ashes of aviation in the United States.

For several years, America had lagged behind the rest of the world in the progress of commercial aviation. Lindbergh's personality, backed by his expressed conviction of the future of the airplane as a transport vehicle, and now his demonstration that anything was possible, combined to awaken the nation. During the next two years, the United States overhauled every other country in the world in its airline activity, and then went on to dominate. Charles Lindbergh's 1927 flight, augmented by later sorties narrated in this book, were an important factor in this process.

Crowds and More Crowds

After what must have been, for Charles Lindbergh, a long rest, and after receiving much acclamation in Paris, he visited Belgium on 28 May, where he met King Albert and Queen Elizabeth; and flew on to London the next day. He spent five days there, meeting King George V and Queen Mary, as well as the Prince of Wales; then returned to France on an English airplane. The *Spirit of St. Louis,* meanwhile, was dismantled by the Royal Air Force, crated, and placed on board the U.S. cruiser *Memphis* at Gosport. It returned to the United States and unloaded pilot and plane at Norfolk, Virginia. Charles went to New York immediately, on 13 June, to be greeted with unprecedented scenes of ceremony, celebration, and adulation. The tickertape parade in New York was one that has never been matched before or since, as was the previous welcome in New York Harbor, where he transferred from Grover Loening's Air Yacht on to the *Macom,* New York City's official yacht.

Charles was, of course, warmly received by pilots as well as by politicians. He is photographed here with members of the French Air Force, in front of a Nieuport 29C biplane.

The great flight captured the imagination everywhere. When, after a few days rest, he flew the Spirit, via Belgium, to England, an enormous crowd was there to greet him as he landed at Croydon Airport on 29 May. He had to take off again before the end of the landing roll, to avoid injuring the crowd, which had broken through police lines.

The Big Parades

Not since the victory parade of 1918 had Paris seen anything quite like it. As a guest of honor, Charles Lindbergh was driven on a ceremonial parade around the French capital, and is seen here stopping the traffic at the Place de la Concorde.

New York welcomed the Conquering Hero in style. At the harbor, when he arrived, an estimated 500 boats and ships, of all shapes and sizes, escorted him on board the Macom, offical yacht of the Mayor of New York, James J. Walker. Charles had flown from Washington in an Army pursuit 'plane to Mitchel Field, transferred to a Navy amphibian, and boarded the Macom in the Narrows.

Everywhere Charles went, there were welcoming crowds. This picture is believed to have been taken at Floyd Bennett Field. The banner in the crowd advertises the oil used by the 'Lone Eagle.'

New York's Victory Parade for Charles Lindbergh far exceeded in statistics anything before or since. Estimates of the size of the crowd along the route varied between 3 and 4 million. Cleaning up the ticker tape the next day cost the city more than $16,000.

The Goodwill Tour . . .

The Spirit of Goodwill
Backed by Harry Guggenheim, and responding to a nation-wide wave of enthusiastic hero-worship, Charles Lindbergh then took the *Spirit of St Louis* on a tour, in which he managed, from 20 July to 23 October 1927, to visit every one of the 48 States. Except for a diversion because of dense fog on 24 July, he kept on schedule throughout the journey. To avoid the danger of surging crowds which could have endangered life and limb as he landed, another aircraft preceded him along the route, to ensure that the local authorities were prepared for the hero's welcome; and that the near-disastrous crowd scenes in Paris and London would not be repeated.

The Statistics
The total flying time for the 22,000-mile tour was 260 hr 45 min. There were 97 individual take-offs and landings. While this was quite an achievement, often forgotten is that, of the 50 largest metropolitan areas of the United States, the *Spirit* omitted only nine, the main exceptions being Houston, San Antonio, and Miami—too far to the south; while the others were near other larger ones that Charles did visit.

Special Guests
Some of the flights were short local hops, for special people, such as Charles's mother (at Grand Rapids); Henry and Edsel Ford (at Detroit); B.F. Mahoney, builder of the *Spirit* (at San Diego); Harry Guggenheim, Virginia Governor Harry Byrd, and C.C. Maidment (Wright engine representative) at Richmond; Donald Keyhoe (see above) at Oklahoma City, and Milburn Kusterer, on arrival at Mitchel Field, Long Island.

Sentimental Journeys
When stopping at Dayton, he had gone to the Wright airfield, to acknowledge the heritage of the Whirlwind engine that had never let him down. He had retraced the route between Chicago and St. Louis that he himself had planned for the air mail. He had stopped at Little Falls, Minnesota, where he had grown up, and hardened himself for the rigors of interminable flying and resistance against all weathers. No doubt, across the plains and the prairies, he was reminded of his barnstorming adventures, only a few years earlier. Now, in this tour, and the epic flight that preceded it, he signalled the end of the barnstorming era and demonstrated that the airplane was meant to carry people, and not just the mail.

All Work—But Some Play
Occasionally, as shown on the map, Charles Lindbergh took a break from the routine of receptions and parades. He seldom took a bee-line between stops, always flying low over intermediate communities, often dropping leaflets to promote the idea of air travel. Sometimes, he made a well-earned diversion, for example, in Montana, where, for sheer pleasure, he and a blithe *Spirit* viewed some of the nation's national parks.

Courtesy Calls
The Hero went to Washington on 16 June, to collect his precious steed at Bolling Field, and flew it back to Mitchel Field, Long Island, whence he made a 9 hr 20 min flight to St. Louis on the next day, to show his sponsors that their faith had not been wasted. Leaving the *Spirit* at St. Louis, he went to Washington, D.C., on 20 June, to meet President Coolidge, and then on to Dayton, Ohio, home of the Wright brothers, on 22 June. Within one month, he had been the guest—and an honoured one at that—of four Heads of State: not bad for a 25-year-old air mail pilot.

Relaxation at Last
Charles was then invited to be the house guest of Harry Guggenheim, the wealthy industrialist, philanthropist, and aviation supporter (via the Guggenheim Foundation) at the secluded estate on Long Island, where he was able, finally, to relax, to write, to contemplate, and to recover from a series of public events that was testing even his indomitable stamina.

On his goodwill tour of the United States, Charles Lindbergh was given a true hero's welcome at every stop he made. These pictures illustrate a typical motorized escort across the airfield, amid enthusiastic applause. (Courtesy: J.M. Mitchelhill)

The Spirit of St. Louis *takes a rest (believed to be at an airfield in Missouri) while Charles Lindbergh is honored by the local populace.*

... of the 48 States

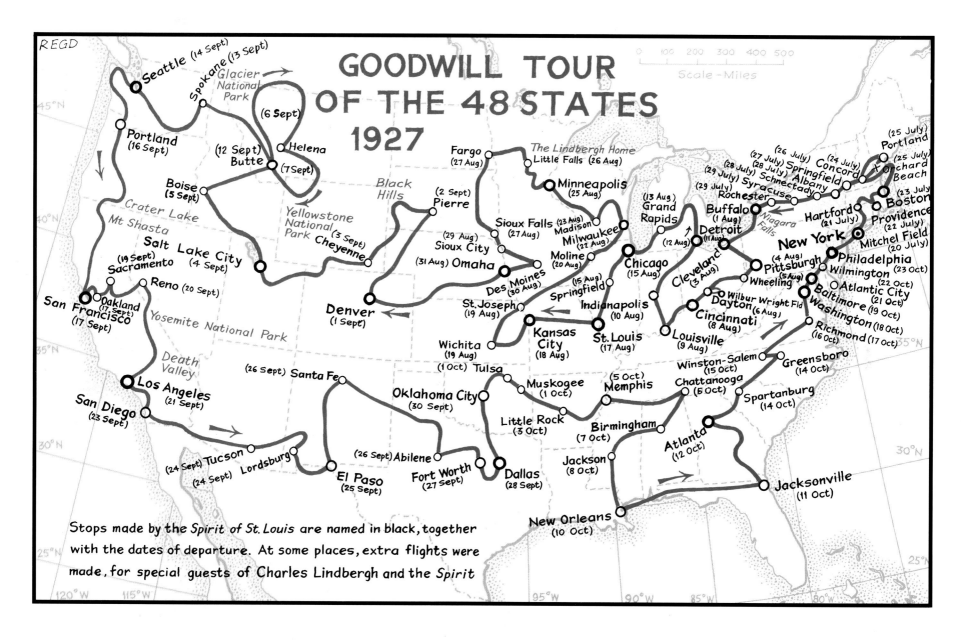

REGD

GOODWILL TOUR OF THE 48 STATES 1927

Scale—Miles
0 100 200 300 400 500

Seattle (14 Sept)
Spokane (13 Sept)
Glacier National Park
(6 Sept)
Portland (16 Sept)
(12 Sept) Butte
Helena
(7 Sept)
Boise (5 Sept)
Yellowstone National Park (3 Sept)
Black Hills
Fargo (27 Aug)
The Lindbergh Home
Little Falls (26 Aug)
Minneapolis (25 Aug)
(2 Sept) Pierre
Crater Lake
Mt Shasta
Salt Lake City (4 Sept)
Sacramento (19 Sept)
Cheyenne
Sioux Falls (27 Aug)
Madison (23 Aug)
Milwaukee (22 Aug)
(13 Aug) Grand Rapids
Buffalo (1 Aug)
Niagara Falls
(26 July) Concord (25 July)
(27 July) Springfield (24 July) Portland
(28 July) Albany Orchard Beach
(28 July) Schnectady
(29 July) Syracuse
(29 July) Rochester
Hartford (21 July)
Boston (23 July)
Providence (22 July)
Reno (20 Sept)
San Francisco (17 Sept)
Oakland (17 Sept)
Yosemite National Park
Death Valley
(29 Aug) Sioux City
(31 Aug) Omaha
Des Moines (30 Aug)
Moline (20 Aug)
Chicago (15 Aug)
(12 Aug) Detroit (11 Aug)
Cleveland (3 Aug)
Wheeling
Pittsburgh (5 Aug)
New York (4 Aug)
Mitchel Field (20 July)
Philadelphia (23 Oct)
Wilmington
Atlantic City (22 Oct)
Baltimore (21 Oct)
Washington (18 Oct)
Springfield (15 Aug)
St. Joseph (19 Aug)
Indianapolis (10 Aug)
Kansas City (18 Aug)
St. Louis (17 Aug)
Dayton (6 Aug)
Wilbur Wright Fld
Cincinnati (8 Aug)
Louisville (9 Aug)
Richmond (16 Oct)
Los Angeles (21 Sept)
San Diego (23 Sept)
(26 Sept) Santa Fe
Wichita (19 Aug)
(10 Oct) Tulsa
Oklahoma City (30 Sept)
(5 Oct) Muskogee (1 Oct)
Memphis
Winston-Salem (15 Oct)
Chattanooga (5 Oct)
Greensboro (14 Oct)
Spartanburg (14 Oct)
(24 Sept) Tucson
Lordsburg
(24 Sept)
(26 Sept) Abilene
Fort Worth (27 Sept)
El Paso (25 Sept)
Dallas (28 Sept)
Little Rock (3 Oct)
Jackson (8 Oct)
Birmingham (7 Oct)
Atlanta (12 Oct)
Jacksonville (11 Oct)
New Orleans (10 Oct)

Stops made by the *Spirit of St. Louis* are named in black, together with the dates of departure. At some places, extra flights were made, for special guests of Charles Lindbergh and the *Spirit*

El *Espíritu de San Luis*

Friendship with Juan Trippe

Beating the U.S. transcontinental speed record, flying solo across the North Atlantic, and visiting every single one of the then 48 States—all within a period of a few months—would seem to have been enough work for the diminutive *Spirit of St. Louis,* which was built, be it remembered, during a time when aircraft were never expected to last very long, with a couple of years' life regarded as typical, even for an airplane that hardly ventured far beyond its home state. But Charles Lindbergh had one more task to perform, partly self-generated perhaps, partly encouraged by his new-found friend Juan Trippe, whose dream of a Pan American airline empire was beginning to take shape in a mind that in many ways matched Lindbergh's in its agility and breadth of vision.

Caribbean Tour

One of Juan Trippe's first geographically strategic objectives was to encompass the Caribbean Sea, and to adopt the small countries of Central America and the West Indian islands as part of his prospective airline empire. A Lindbergh Goodwill Tour would not only provide all the advance publicity he needed, but Charles's inimitable experience would be priceless in providing technical advice for future planning. And so it was. The *Spirit* did exactly what was expected of it, as shown in the map.

The Spirit Carries the Mail

Towards the end of the Caribbean circumnavigation, the *Spirit* carried mail from Santo Domingo to Haiti and Cuba, possibly the only occasion when that famous airplane carried a payload. This was done at the request of West Indian Aerial Express, an airline founded in Santo Domingo in 1927 and which was later absorbed by Pan American. Special covers were prepared for this event. The one illustrated was addressed to Basil Rowe, WIAE's chief pilot.

Charles Lindbergh and The Spirit of St. Louis *continued their travels together. Early in 1928 he made another goodwill tour, this time encircling the Caribbean Sea. This picture was taken at St. Thomas on 31 January 1928.*

This itinerary—not entirely without incident—was the harbinger of a future airline network—see page 34.

see page 34.

Flight of
El Espíritu de San Luis
1927-28

26

Honorable Retirement

The Spirit of St. Louis, *having been disassembled and transported by road from Bolling Field, is uncrated at the East Door of the Arts and Industries Museum of the Smithsonian Institution in 1928.*

A great day for the Smithsonian: the Spirit *is prepared for hoisting (out of harm's way) on 13 May 1928.*

It took an honored place in 'The Nation's Attic.' Appropriately, the small sign at the hall entrance in the rear stated "History of the United States."

The Ryan NYP, registered as N-X-211, was finally retired. At the suggestion of Paul Garber, C.G. Abbott, the assistant secretary of the Smithsonian Institution, sent a congratulatory telegram to Charles on 23 May 1927. He also had the foresight to suggest that the *Spirit of St. Louis* should be donated to the Smithsonian. And this was agreed. For many years it resided in the Arts and Industries Building on Washington's Mall, until the National Air and Space Museum building was opened in 1976, and where the *Spirit* now hangs in a place of honor, close enough for inspection, but, for the sake of posterity, not close enough to touch.

When the new building opened, the famous aircraft was transferred, with tender loving care, to a new place of honor, in the Milestones of Flight gallery, hanging next to the Wright *Flyer* and other airplanes and space-craft capsules that changed the course of history.

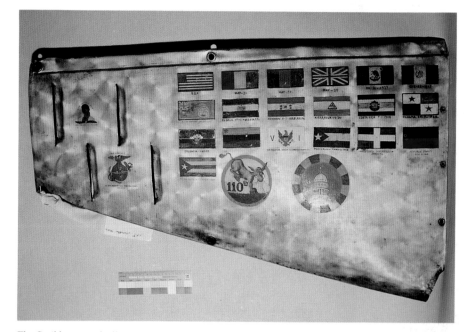

The Caribbean goodwill tour led to the addition of quite a few more flags to the Spirit's *fuselage. This picture was taken of the actual panel when the aircraft was undergoing conservation at the National Air and Space Museum. (photo: E. McManus)*

The country flags are, left to right, from the top: U.S.A. (No date); France, 21 May; Belgium, 28 May; U.K., 29 May; Mexico, 14 Dec.; Guatemala, 28 Dec.; British Honduras, 30 Dec.; El Salvador, l Jan. 1929; Honduras, 3 Jan.; Nicaragua, 5 Jan.; Costa Rica, 7 Jan.; Panama, 9 Jan.; Columbia (sic), 27 Jan.; Venezuela, 29 Jan.; St. Thomas, 31 Jan.; Porto Rico, 2 Feb.; Republica Dominica, 4 Feb.; Haiti, 6 Feb.; Cuba, 8 Feb. On the left are the emblems of the Marine Base at France Field, Panama, and at Bonen Field, Port-au-Prince; and below are those of the Missouri National Guard and Bolling Field, Washington, D.C.

NEBRASKA

UTAH

KANSAS

Legend:

O ... T.W.A. SCHEDULED STOPS

● .... Other airfields (lighted)

○ .... " " " (unlighted)

× ..... Lighted Airway (revolving lighthouse beacon

W .... Weather Reporting Stations

T .... Teletype Service

✠ .... Radio Range

KINGMAN

Seligman (WT)
Seligman (W)
Ashfork (WT)
Mr Bill Williams (W)
Maine (W)
W Flagstaff
Winona

WINSLOW

llers Ranch

Presco ○
Jerome

(WT) Holbrook

Deeplake (WT)
● Gallup (W)

Zuni W ×
El Morro (W)

St Johns ○

Springerville

ARIZONA

(WT) Acomita

Socorro

NEW MEXICO

○ Las Vegas
Dilia (WT)

Otto (WT)

Vaughn W

Cuervo

Tucumari (WT)

Adrian (WT)

ALBUQUERQUE

Clovis

TEXAS

AMARILLO

Canadian

W Glazier (WT)

Pampa (WT)
Shamrock W

(W) Elk City
Mangum

Fargo (WT)

OKLAHOMA

Waynoka (WT)

Winfield

OKLAHOMA CITY

Hobart

Chickasha

Norman ○

Guthrie

Cushing

Chandler ○
Stroud

Bris

(WT) Cassoday
Newton

WICHITA

(WT) Anthony

Planning a Route ... and Spanning a Continent

The original blueprint of this extremely detailed planning map, prepared for the historic Transcontinental & Western Air coast-to-coast route in 1931, was signed by Jack Frye, president of the airline and himself a skilled and experienced pilot. But the concentration of detail bears the hallmark of Lindbergh thoroughness. For in addition to being heavily involved with Pan American as technical advisor (see pages 32–47) Charles was also technical advisor to T.W.A. He was, incidentally, well paid for the formidable task: $10,000 per year, plus 25,000 shares, sold to him at well below market value.

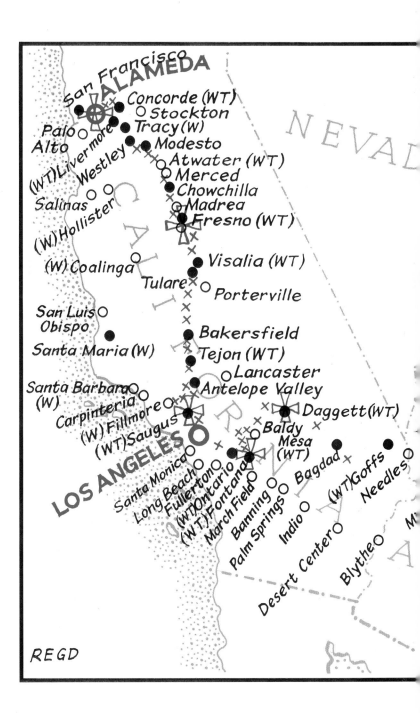

Planning a Route . . .

The Day by Plane ✣ The Night by Train

REDUCE your travel time by half—enjoy the fun of flying—at approximately the cost of rail and Pullman travel.

Transcontinental Air Transport-Maddux Air Lines (The Lindbergh Line), operating in conjunction with the Pennsylvania and Santa Fe railroads, carry you across the continent in two days—half the time ordinarily required. Within intermediate territory this air-rail system saves hours and days for your business and pleasure. The scope of your travel is vastly extended and new places added to your itinerary. Frequent schedules at convenient hours place the dependable service and comfort of this vast system at your disposal daily.

COLONEL CHARLES A. LINDBERGH
Chairman, Technical Committee

TAT-Maddux Air Lines have placed the speed, safety and comfort of air travel and the pure fun of flying within the means of all. Should you travel for business, for pleasure or from necessity, the service of the air-rail system is at your disposal just as are the vast rail systems. For cross-continent journeys, short business trips or vacation tours to the nation's beauty spots, TAT-Maddux provides a fast, dependable service at ordinary travel cost and with great comfort and enjoyment. Daily air and rail connections are available to the Great Southwest, the Midwest and the Northwest. California's beauty and its playgrounds lie a mere two days from the industrial East over the TAT-Maddux system.

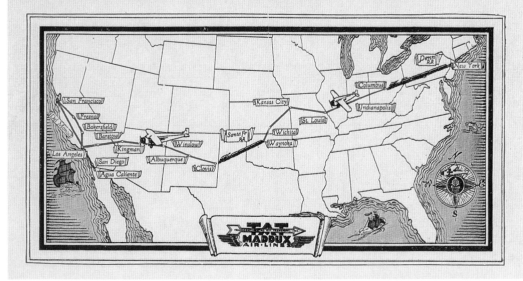

. . . and Spanning a Continent

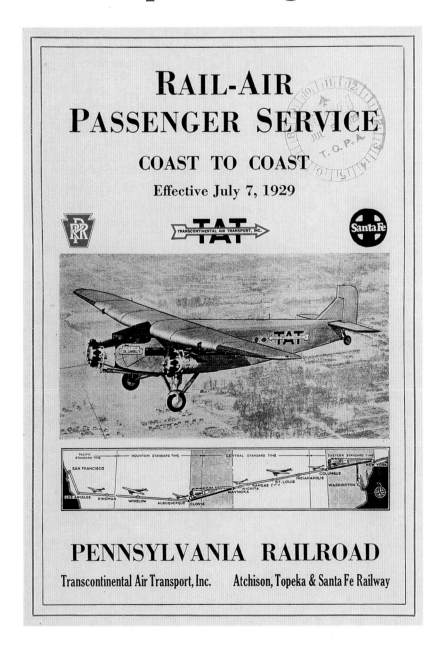

RAIL-AIR
PASSENGER SERVICE

COAST TO COAST

Effective July 7, 1929

PENNSYLVANIA RAILROAD

Transcontinental Air Transport, Inc.   Atchison, Topeka & Santa Fe Railway

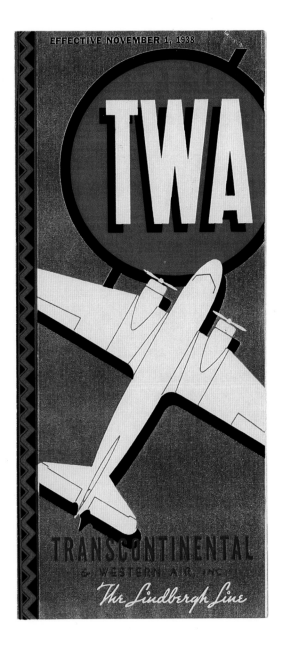

EFFECTIVE NOVEMBER 1, 1938

TWA

TRANSCONTINENTAL
& WESTERN AIR, INC.

The Lindbergh Line

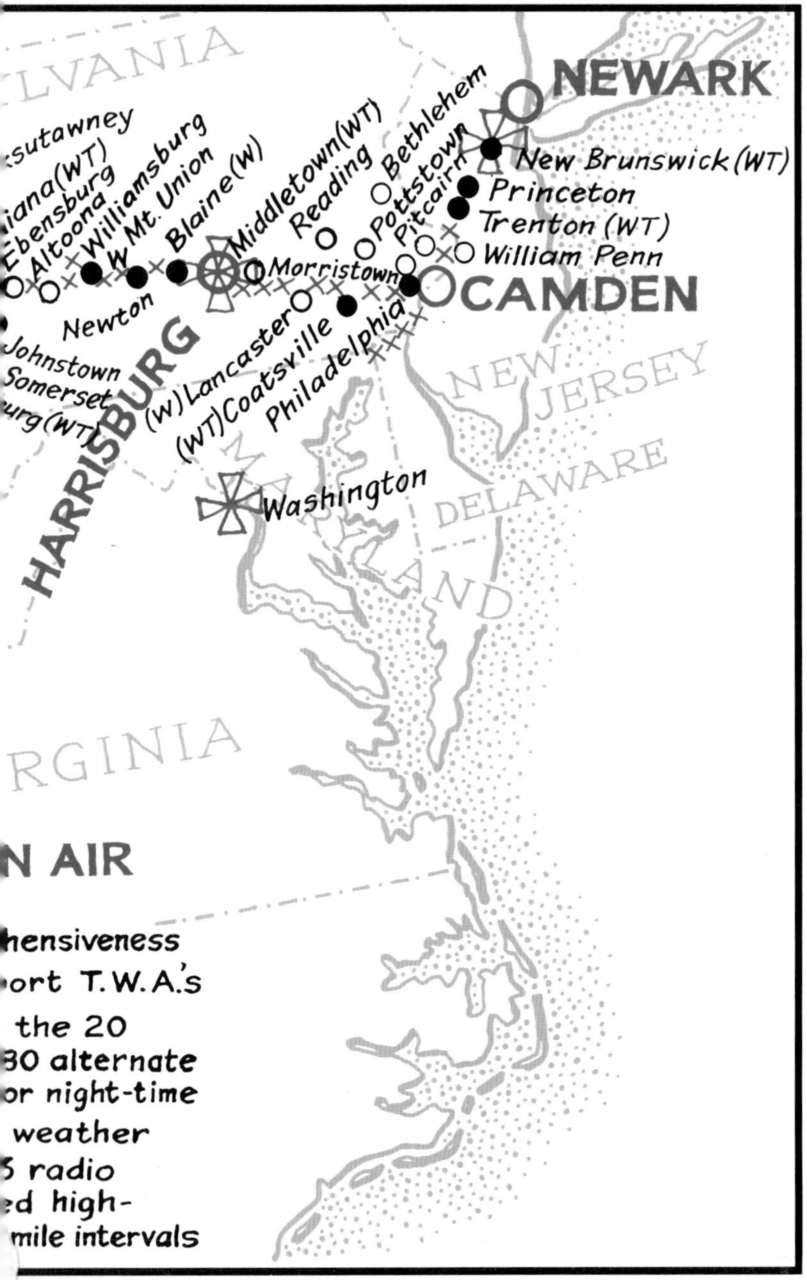

Map labels:

PENNSYLVANIA (partial: ...LVANIA)

...sutawney
...iana(WT)
...Ebensburg
Altoona
Williamsburg
W. Mt. Union
Blaine(w)
Middletown(WT)
Reading
Bethlehem
Pottstown
Pitcairn
Newton
Johnstown
Somerset
...urg(WT)
HARRISBURG
Morristown
(w)Lancaster
(WT)Coatsville
Philadelphia
Washington

NEWARK
New Brunswick (WT)
Princeton
Trenton (WT)
William Penn
CAMDEN

NEW JERSEY
DELAWARE
MARYLAND
VIRGINIA (partial: ...RGINIA)

...N AIR

...hensiveness
...ort T.W.A.'s
...the 20
...30 alternate
...or night-time
...weather
...radio
...d high-
...mile intervals

The Lindbergh Line

In 1930, at the insistence of Postmaster General Walter Folger Brown, who was averse to the idea of awarding lucrative mail contracts to more than one airline on any mainline route, forced the merger of the two aspirants for the coast-to-coast route between Los Angeles and New York. Western Air Express thus merged with Transcontinental Air Transport, to become Transcontinental & Western Air (T.W.A.). The airline adopted the slogan *The Lindbergh Line,* after its famous technical advisor, and continued to use it until December 1939, when the great hero's political views differed from those of the government.

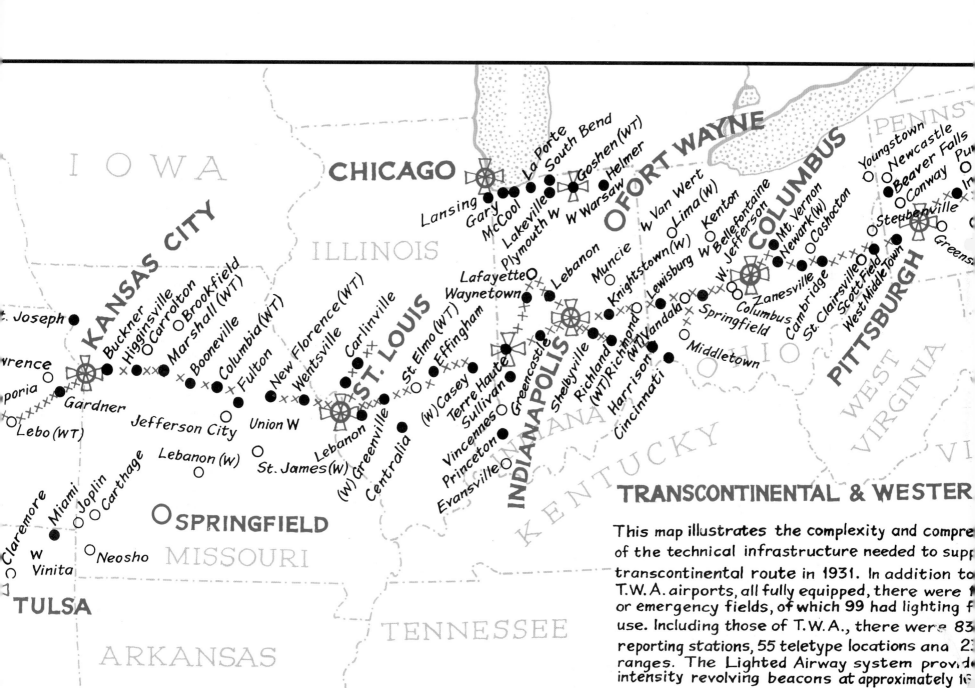

IOWA

CHICAGO

KANSAS CITY

ILLINOIS

O FORT WAYNE

COLUMBUS

PITTSBURGH

St. Joseph

Buckner
Higginsville
Carrolton
Brookfield
Marshall (WT)
Booneville
Columbia (WT)
Fulton
New Florence (WT)
Wentsville
Carlinville
ST. LOUIS
St. Elmo (WT)
Effingham
Waynetown
Lafayette
Lebanon
Muncie
W Van Wert
Lima (W)
Kenton
W Bellefontaine
W Jefferson
Mt. Vernon
Newark (W)
Coshocton
Zanesville
Cambridge
St. Clairsville
Scott Field
West Middletown
Steubenville
Greensb

Lansing
Gary
McCool
Lakeville
Plymouth W
W Warsaw
Helmer
Goshen (WT)

Youngstown
Newcastle
Beaver Falls
Conway
Pu
In

La Porte
South Bend

rence
poria
Gardner
Lebo (WT)
Jefferson City
Union W
Lebanon
(W) Greenville
Centralia
St. James (W)
(W) Casey
Terre Haute
Sullivan
Vincennes
Princeton
Evansville
INDIANAPOLIS
Shelbyville
Richland
Richmond (WT)
Harrison
Vandala
Cincinnati
Greencastle
Knightstown (W)
Lewisburg
W
Springfield
Columbus
Middletown

Claremore
Miami
Joplin
Carthage
Lebanon (W)
W
Vinita
Neosho

SPRINGFIELD

MISSOURI

KENTUCKY

OHIO

WEST VIRGINIA

VI

TULSA

TENNESSEE

ARKANSAS

TRANSCONTINENTAL & WESTER

This map illustrates the complexity and compre
of the technical infrastructure needed to supp
transcontinental route in 1931. In addition to
T.W.A. airports, all fully equipped, there were
or emergency fields, of which 99 had lighting f
use. Including those of T.W.A., there were 83
reporting stations, 55 teletype locations and 2
ranges. The Lighted Airway system provide
intensity revolving beacons at approximately 1

Transcontinental Air Transport

As technical consultant to the pioneering Transcontinental Air Transport (T.A.T.) Charles Lindbergh was no desk-bound executive. He was active in the survey work and planning (see pages 28–29) and was on hand to take the left-hand seat of the inaugural eastbound Ford Tri-Motor on 8 July 1929. The crowd was entertained by a preliminary display of ten training 'circuits and bumps' to comply with the regulatory letter of the law.

The T.A.T. transcontinental route was an elaborate affair, demanding much planning, organization, and structural work. At Columbus, Ohio, a special rail-air transfer station was built. The mainline Pennsylvania Railroad tracks are in the background of this picture. The actual building at 'Port Columbus' is still there today.

By this time, Charles Lindbergh was both hero and celebrity, sought after by the rich and famous as well as by the millions of average Americans. On the occasion of the T.A.T. inaugural, Charles and Anne posed with film stars Mary Pickford and (far left) Douglas Fairbanks.

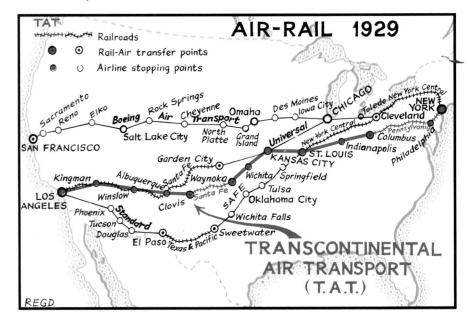

Rail and Air, 1929

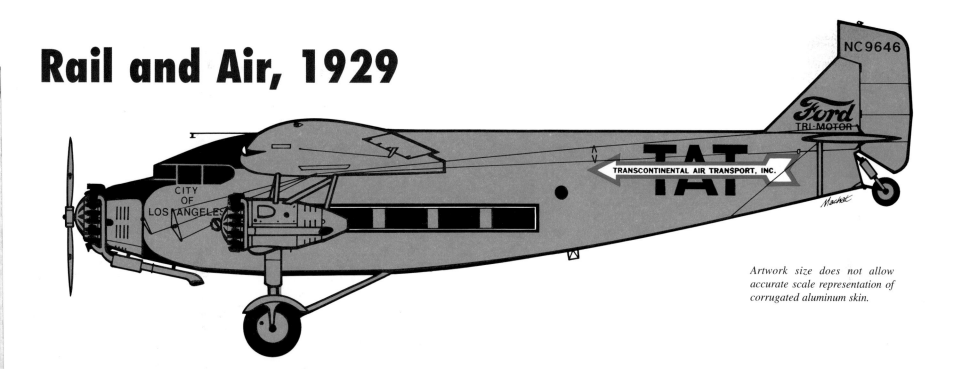

Artwork size does not allow accurate scale representation of corrugated aluminum skin.

Ford 5-AT Tri-Motor

Length/Span:	.50/78 feet
Engine	.3 x Pratt & Whitney Wasp (420 hp)
Passenger Seats	.13
Cruise Speed	.100 mph
MGTOW	.13,500 lb
Normal Range	.560 st. miles

To state that Charles Lindbergh could fly any airplane at any time (within its technical limitations), and anywhere, was no exaggeration. And so he upgraded himself from flimsy single-engined types to the heavier all-metal transports without apparent effort. He flew the famous Ford Tri-Motor 'Tin Goose' for both Pan Am and T.A.T., notably on several inaugurals.

He was famously pictured at Port Columbus, the rail-air transfer station in Ohio, during the time when the routes across the two main mountain chains was considered too dangerous; and also at Los Angeles, for the eastbound inaugural. This latter was marred by the little-publicised event when the pilot flying the companion airplane (the inaugural was flown in several sections) arrived at Kingman, the destination airfield, before the famous Lindy.

Of the several group pictures taken in July 1929, for the T.A.T. inaugural (see page 30), this one is interesting in that it includes (6th from left) an upcoming aviatrix, Miss Amelia Earhart, as well as Charles, conspicuously tall, and Anne Lindbergh next to him.

Pan American Pilot, 1929

Mexican Inaugural

Towards the end of 1927, Charles Lindbergh had renewed his association with the airline business. He became a friend of Juan Trippe, president of Pan American Airways, and took an active role as technical advisor. He flew some of Pan Am's airplanes, demonstrating a talent for route proving and surveying, and, by participating in inaugurals, acting as a prestigious promoter. Incidentally, he was in great demand in this role—see pages 28–31.

His first mission for Pan Am was to the Ford Tri-Motor fly from Brownsville, Texas, to Mexico City, on 10 March 1929. In the airline's ambitious and visionary plans for expansion, it had acquired Compañía Mexicana de Avación (C.M.A.), thus overcoming problems of national sovereignty and traffic rights. Lindbergh's inaugural flight has always fascinated philatelists, because of some mail that was mislaid for three weeks, either because it was unloaded and ignored, amid the concentration on the Hero, rather than on the airplane or its cargo; or because it was still inside the wing compartment, and no-one in Mexico was aware of its existence.

The Versatile Ford

The Ford Tri-Motor was the flagship of all self-respecting American airlines during the closing years of the 1920s and until 1933, when the first 'modern' airliner, the Boeing 247, appeared, and promptly made all other transport airplanes obsolescent, at least in the United States. Most of the Fords then found a home in the countries of Central America, where they performed some amazing feats of cargo carrying into primitive airstrips in almost impenetrable jungles.

Lindbergh and Ford

Charles Lindbergh's connection with the Ford company was sustained. He was born in Detroit in 1902. On 11 August 1927, he took Henry Ford for his first airplane ride—in the *Spirit*, no less. Charles indirectly promoted the Ford Tri-Motor with both T.A.T./T.W.A. (pages 28–31) and Pan American (this and opposite page). Later, when he was *persona non grata* with the political establishment at the outbreak of the Second World War, Henry Ford helped Charles to channel his talents towards the war effort (see page 50).

Lindbergh's inaugural Ford flight.

Brownsville

0 100 200 300
Scale-Miles

Tampico

MEXICO CITY

Mexican Inaugural
10 March 1929

REGD

Charles Lindbergh was as much at home with large aircraft as with small ones. Here he is with Pan American's first Fokker tri-motor, in the fall of 1927. The Series F.VIIa/3m was christened after the Assistant Postmaster General of the time.

This was the scene at the airport in Mexico City when Charles Lindbergh brought in the first substantial load of air mail flown from the U.S.A. Excitement must have been high as the ground crew did not wait for the engines to stop.

The Tin Goose Again

Artwork size does not allow accurate scale representation of corrugated aluminum skin.

Ford 5-AT Tri-Motor

Length/Span:	.50/78 feet
Engines	.3 x Pratt & Whitney Wasp (420 hp)
Passenger Seats	.13
Cruise Speed	.100 mph
MGTOW	.13,500 lb
Normal Range	.560 st. miles

A Long Life

The first Ford Tri-Motor, a Wright Whirlwind-powered Model 4-AT, first flew at Dearborn, Michigan, on 11 June 1926. A later version, the Model 5-AT, had the more powerful Pratt & Whitney Wasp engines. By June 1933, when the last one came off the line, a total of 205 had been built, and until the Boeing 247 heralded a new generation of fast modern airliners in 1933, it reigned supreme in the U.S. airline world. Such was its rugged metal construction that, even today, one or two of these vintage aircraft are still in flying condition.

The Ford Tri-Motor became the flagship of Mexico's national flag carrier, Compañía Mexicana de Aviación (C.M.A.), linking the capital city with gateway junction points at the U.S. border, and also with the countries of Central America. This aircraft is a Ford 4-AT.

Caribbean Sorties, 1929–30

More than Goodwill ....

Charles Lindbergh's trip around the Caribbean in the *Spirit* (see page 26) had been something of an adventure, but it was also something of an education. While instinctively favoring landplanes, he had, on that journey, realized that their operation on a regular and continuous basis depended upon the preparation and maintenance of good airfields. And in the heavily forested and often mountainous terrain of Central America, these qualities were difficult to attain. In contributing technical advice to Pan American Airways, he was once again paid handsomely, in similar vein to the arrangements with T.A.T. (pages 28–30) but this time he advocated the use of flying boats.

Waterborne Advantages

A small seaplane could alight on any stretch of smooth water, on the coast, or in a coastal lagoon, on a lake, and even on a river: any smooth surface of water that could be kept clear of obstructions, such as floating debris, or even small craft. This was invariably easier to do than to persuade the local farmers to drive their cattle from a nicely cleared slice of jungle which did not seem to be used very much—just a visiting 'plane every second day or so.

Pan Am Encircles the Caribbean

During a period of only a few months, the theory became accomplished fact. The ideal little flying boat was found (see opposite page) and the Pan American presence was quickly established. The rapid progress is shown on the accompanying map, which also plots the extension to Paramaribo, on 23 September 1929. This tentacle of route expansion was only just the beginning of Juan Trippe's and Pan American's dominance of the airways of Latin America.

The Sikorsky S-38

This versatile little amphibian, the Sikorsky S-38, went into service, first with the New York, Rio & Buenos Aires Line (NYRBA) in July 1928, and with Pan American Airways three months later. Powered by two Pratt and Whitney Wasp engines (450 horse power each) and well constructed of wood and metal framework, with doped fabric covering, it could carry eight passengers. Lightly loaded, it could fly over a range of about 500 miles, but normally it would be confined to distances of 200–300 miles, quite sufficient for the island-

The Sikorsky S-38 was a snug little flying boat, as portrayed opposite; and was one of the few commercial aircraft in which passengers had to enter or leave through the roof. In this picture, taken in British Guiana in 1929, Charles Lindbergh and Juan Trippe appear to be contemplating a little wing-walking.

hopping routes around the Caribbean Sea, where it pioneered Pan American's early expansion beyond the vicinity of Florida and Cuba.

Of the total of 101 S-38s built, Pan American ordered no less than 27. Charles Lindbergh had played a part in selecting it, and was active in monitoring its development. They were to be found as far south as Montevideo, and some were sent to China, for Pan Am's subsidiary airline there, to operate, albeit briefly, along the coastal route.

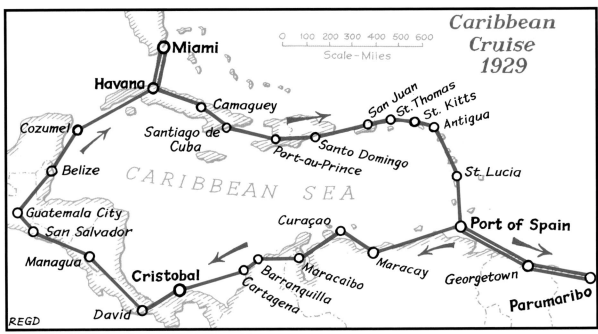

In 1929, the Lindberghs and the Trippes went on an aerial cruise that, for them, was both a triumph of achievement in making a survey of the Caribbean for Pan American Airways, and, at the same time, an exciting holiday cruise.

Versatile Flying Boat

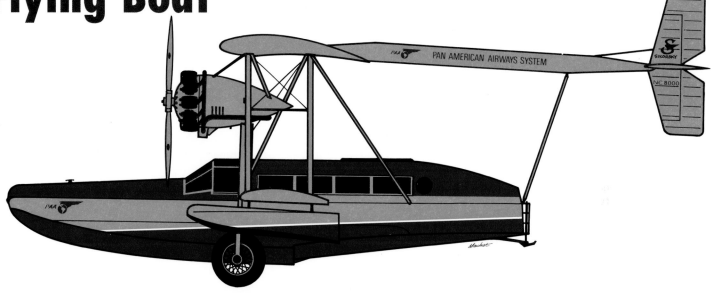

Sikorsky S-38

Length/Span:	.......40/72 feet
Engines	......2 x Pratt & Whitney Wasp (420 hp)
Passenger Seats	8
Cruise Speed	..........110 mph
MGTOW	.............10,480 lb
Normal Range	.......600 st. miles

Designer Igor Sikorsky called this airplane the Amphibion.

The S-38 seemed to wallow in the water before getting airborne, and though, by modern standards, a bit of an ugly duckling, it performed reliably and well, and enabled Pan American Airways to establish itself firmly in the Caribbean and Central American countries (courtesy: Denis Wrynn collection).

Fitted with comfortable padded seats, the first-class interior of the S-38 drew few complaints (left). Normally, however, in keeping with the requirements for tropical conditions, long before the introduction of air conditioning, wicker seats were standard (right).

Short-Cut to Panama, 1931

Direct Flight to the Canal

The Consolidated Commodore, (of which type Pan American had acquired a fleet of 14 aircraft in 1930 when it acquired the complete assets of the New York, Rio, & Buenos Aires Line (NYRBA)) had already demonstrated the advantage of its 800-mile range by making the first direct flights from Miami to Panama (Cristobal), via Jamaica, in 1929.

The First Clipper

Then, on 19 November 1931, in a dramatic inaugural, Pan American introduced the four-engined Sikorsky S-40 on the trans-Caribbean service. The aircraft could seat 38 passengers in a hitherto unattainable standard of comfort. It had three times the capacity of the biggest U.S. landplane of the period; and Juan Trippe and Charles Lindbergh, together with their wives, were there for the occasion. The event was also marked by Pan Am's adoption of the brand-name 'Clipper' for all its aircraft. The S-40 was the first of a long line.

An Hour of Glory

Dramatic though the introduction of the 38-seat giant was—and it attracted enormous publicity at the Dinner Key Pan American flying boat base in Miami—the influence of the Sikorsky S-40 was not extensive. For although it was able to provide a good service to Panama, and a luxurious one for the passengers, it was soon superseded by a better aircraft. The agile designer, Igor Sikorsky, working with Charles Lindbergh as Pan American's technical advisor, had a successor on the drawing boards even as the S-40 took to the waters. The S-42 was not bigger, but it had much cleaner lines, without the ungainly tail booms, or the web of wiring, and the engines were faired into the wings. The S-42 was about 40% faster than the S-40, and had more range; and as a result only three S-40s were built. But it did its job on the Panama route, and was not retired until the Second World War.

Forerunner of the big Sikorsky was the elegant Consolidated Commodore, introduced by the New York, Rio & Buenos Aires Line (NYRBA) which was taken over by Pan American. It was the first commercial aircraft to take the 'short cut' to Panama. (photo: United Technologies)

This picture was taken when the 40-seat Sikorsky S-40 was towed gently into the dock at Barranquilla, Colombia during the early 1930s. Charles Lindbergh had previously visited this marine terminal (of SCADTA, the ancestor of the present-day AVIANCA) on survey flights with the Trippes

(Left) The S-40 was able to offer greater comfort than any other airliner of its time.

This map shows how the curcuitous route to the Panama Canal Zone was shortened, first by the Commodore, then by the Sikorsky S-40.

The S-40 was able to carry far greater loads of air freight and express cargo than could any previous transport aircraft.

The First Clipper

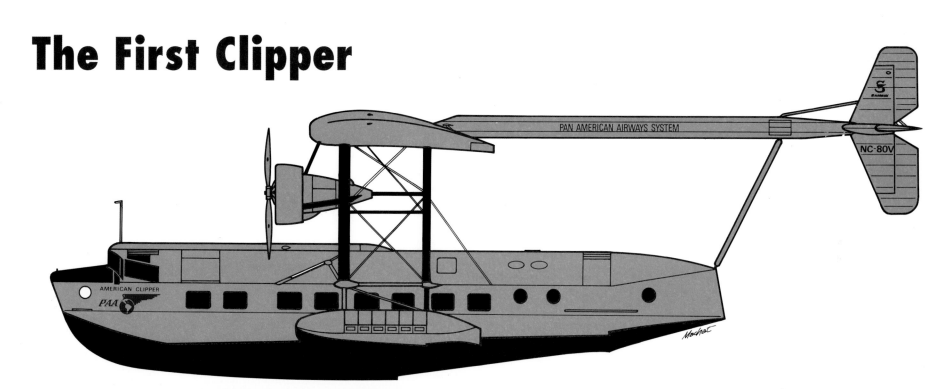

PAN AMERICAN AIRWAYS SYSTEM

NC-80V

AMERICAN CLIPPER

PAA

Sikorsky S-40

Length/Span: . . . . .77/114 feet	Passenger Seats .38	Cruise speed . . . . .115 mph
Engine . . .4 x Pratt & Whitney Hornet (575 hp)	MGTOW .34,000 lb	Normal Range . . . . .900 st. miles

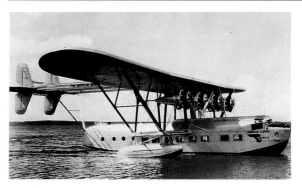

The Sikorsky S-40, looking quite business-like in this picture, was the first of Pan American's big flying boats to be called Clippers.

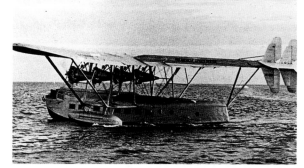

Photographers liked to take pictures of the Sikorsky S-40. But from whatever angle, it was difficult to conceal the array of struts and wires that led cynics to describe the aircraft as "a collection of parts flying in close formation."

The Lindberghs . . .

Good Friends

The friendship established between the Lindberghs and the Trippes was solid. Charles and Anne returned to the United States in 1939, became involved in the America First movement, and were then engulfed by the outbreak of war. Juan Trippe would have liked to have brought him into the Pan American organization at a high level. But even Trippe was unable to help, because of the powerful political implications (see page 50). Charles had curtly declined to serve as chairman of the Civil Aeronautics Authority (C.A.A.), and he was not on speaking terms with the President of the United States. And so Trippe was in a difficult position. After the war was over, however, Charles Lindbergh became a director of Pan American, and was able to offer to Trippe the sound advice of an Elder Statesman.

Charles Lindbergh, the veteran Robertson air mail pilot, was still available when needed with Pan American. He is seen here, pilot's helmet in hand, with (left to right) Glenn Curtiss, the Mayor of Miami, John Hambleton (co-pilot), and the Miami Postmaster.

This photograph is a minor classic, as it shows Charles and Anne Lindbergh, and Juan and Betty Trippe, as they prepared to take off in a Sikorsky S-38 on the proving flight from San Juan to Paramaribo, Dutch Guiana, in September 1929 (see map, page 34). They were all still in their late twenties.

The mail loaded, helmet on, the pilot prepares to take off with the Sikorsky S-38, here equipped as an amphibian. The wheels could be retracted into the fuselage when used as a flying boat.

. . . and the Trippes

By 1929, two great aviation leaders were firm friends. This picture was taken in Panama, during a Fokker F-10A survey flight.

At that time, Anne Morrow Lindbergh, only recently married, was beginning to adapt to the aviation life. On the early trips to the Caribbean, she was enjoying the ride, as a passenger; but within two years she became a competent navigator/radio operator (see pages 40–41 and 44–45).

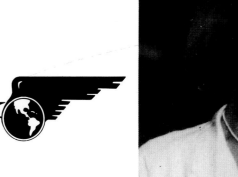

Wherever Lindbergh went, the cameras followed. In this picture the Lindberghs and the Trippes are preparing for a flight in a Fokker F-10A.

Great Circle to the Orient, 1931

The Lindbergh Team

Juan Trippe was Pan American's inspiration and presiding visionary. Charles Lindbergh was Pan Am's resident trailblazer and one-man survey team. Or, to be correct, Mr. and Mrs. Lindbergh were the team, for everywhere that Lindbergh went, his wife Anne, was sure to go. No one had expected this little lady—her diminutive stature emphasized by Charles's height—would, for many years, be his constant companion on many exploratory and stamina-demanding journeys. Furthermore, she was no mere companion, just along for the ride. She taught herself radio and navigational skills that could match those of any professional.

North to the Orient

Anne was also an accomplished writer. Her diaries complemented those of her husband, documenting the magnificent survey flights that were to prove invaluable to Trippe and Pan Am in the formidable ambition of conquering both the Pacific and the Atlantic Oceans. Her *North to the Orient* tells the epic story of how they flew from New York to China, via Alaska and the fringes of northeastern Siberia, the Kurile Islands, and Japan, and the Ruyukyu Islands, to establish the operational practicability of the shortest route to the Orient.

In the event, the survey flight was redundant. The operational problems, particularly those associated with the uncertain and often treacherous meteorological conditions of the Arctic north, and especially the constant mists and fogs of the Aleutian island chain, proved to be a hazard. Also, the political conditions were far from encouraging, as the Soviet Union was only just about to achieve diplomatic recognition by the United States.

Meanwhile, the aircraft manufacturers of large flying boats were making impressive advances in building new Clippers, with long, even trans-ocean range. Juan Trippe was able to cut across the mid-Pacific, taking in the potentially lucrative Honolulu in his stride, and, with Guam and the Philippines under the U.S. flag, he could reach his oriental goal without risk of frigid climates, either according to the temperature or the political thermometer.

These two maps illustrate the advantage of the Great Circle routeing. On a Mercator map projection, the Lindbergh's flight appears circuitous; but the same route plotted on a globe deviates very little from a straight line.

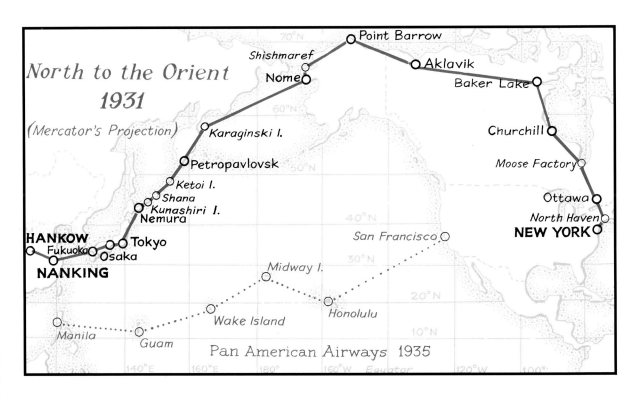

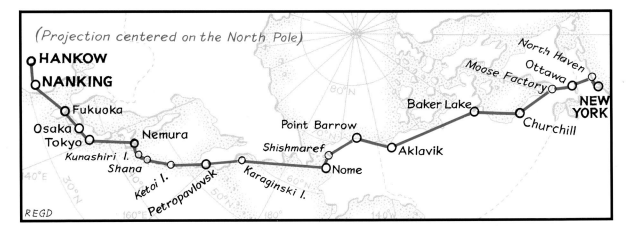

Floatplane Triumph

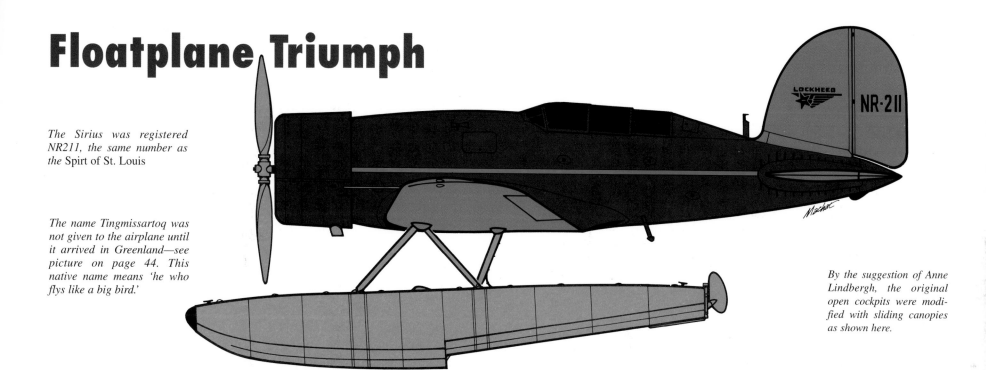

The Sirius was registered NR211, the same number as the *Spirt of St. Louis*

The name *Tingmissartoq* was not given to the airplane until it arrived in Greenland—see picture on page 44. This native name means 'he who flys like a big bird.'

By the suggestion of Anne Lindbergh, the original open cockpits were modified with sliding canopies as shown here.

Lockheed Sirius

Length/Span: . . . . .30/43 feet	Seating . . . . .2 incl. pilot	Cruise speed . . . . .115 mph
Engine . . . . .Wright Cyclone (575 hp–1931, China; 710 hp–1933, Atlantic)	MGTOW . . . . .7,700 lb	Normal Range . . . . .2,100 st. miles

This picture shows Charles and Anne, already a fine flying partnership, boarding the Lockheed Sirius before modification of the cockpit canopies, at Anne Lindbergh's suggestion.

After modification, the Lindberghs were better protected from the elements; and possibly the aerodynamic adjustment helped to improve the aircraft's performance.

This picture of the Lindberghs was taken at College Point, Long Island, in July 1931, as they prepared for their long-distance flight to the Orient.

A Great Airplane

The tall 'Slim' Lindbergh stands out among the smaller Alaskans, while Anne is apparently honored in a ceremonial sled, complete with fittings (but no seat belt). The Sirius and its crew must have been in striking contrast as a mode of transport, compared with sleds on land and kayaks on water.

Floatplane Triumph

The Lockheed company had specialized in building fast, efficient, single-engined aircraft, named after bright stars of the night skies. The Sirius was one of this great line.

The flight to the Orient would be of considerable magnitude with a small airplane, even today. The jets can do so with a certain confidence that supporting installations, repair shops, supplies of spare parts, fuel, and other necessities, can be available almost anywhere on the globe. Back in 1931, when the Lindberghs took the Sirius to China, this was not so. They were forced to be self-supporting, at least beyond Anchorage or Nome. They reached Hankow, up the Yangtse River, without mishap, a great tribute to both aircraft and crew.

While at Hankow, the Lindberghs tried to assist in relief operations for flood victims of the overflowing Yangtse River. But their efforts were curtailed when the Sirius was damaged while being lowered from the Royal Navy's aircraft carrier *HMS Hermes,* which was able to act as a depot ship at the end of the arduous journey.

This picture, of Charles and Anne, all dressed up and a long way to go, with the faithful Sirius as a backdrop, captures the personal, almost romantic aspects of this great man-and-wife crew.

The Sirius on board the British aircraft carrier Hermes, *on the Yangtse River in China.*

During the epic flight to the Orient, the Lindberghs stopped in Japan. This picture was taken at Kasumi-ga-Ura (Tokyo) where Charles seems to be showing some concern for the condition of the pontoons (floats). They stayed in Tokyo from 26 August to 13 September 1931.

And Some Others

This Mahoney (Ryan) B-1X (NX-4215), pictured at Roosevelt Field, was a gift to Charles Lindbergh from Mahoney when the Spirit was donated to the Smithsonian Institution. Charles used it for survey flights from April to October 1928. (Courtesy: David Ostrowski Collection)

In 1934, Charles bought a Monocoupe for his private use. He did not like it very much, because of its tendency to ground loop, and would not allow anyone else to fly it. He donated it to the Missouri Historical Society, and it is on display today at the terminal of St. Louis International Airport. (Courtesy: Fred Ross)

Charles Lindbergh favoured landplanes over floatplanes, but chose the latter when airfields were not available. On 22 May 1929 he was flying a Loening amphibian Air Yacht.

Charles Lindbergh seldom seemed to be away from airplanes for very long. He is pictured here at the Los Angeles National Air Races in 1928 with (left to right) Art Goebel, and Otto and Wally Timm.

This picture was taken at the Cleveland Air Races in 1929. On the left is Lt. Frank O'Bierne, and on the right is Lt. F.N. Kivette, members of an aerobatic team in which Charles Lindbergh participated.

Personal Tragedy . . .

The Kidnapping

The Lindberghs' first child, Charles Jr., was born on 22 June 1930. Then, when Anne was pregnant with their second child, the young Charles was kidnapped in dramatic fashion from their home in New Jersey. After the child was found dead on 12 May 1932, a manhunt began, one that could have made a good detective story, and eventually, after an exhaustive investigation, Bruno Richard Hauptmann, a German immigrant of a few years standing, was arrested.

The trial began on 3 January 1935. Hauptmann was found guilty, and went to the electric chair on 3 April 1936. During the entire period, the Lindberghs were subjected to a disgusting exhibition of press harrassment to the extent that Charles acquired a justifiable antipathy to publicity, a trait in his character that was to stay with him for the rest of his life.

The Atlantic Once Again

When the tragedy of what became known as the affair of the Lindbergh Baby occurred in 1932, Charles and Anne had not long returned from their flight to China (pages 40-42). They had wished to complete a round-the-world itinerary—echoing von Gronau's trips in his Dornier Wal—but the Lockheed Sirius had been damaged while being lowered from the British aircraft carrier *Hermes* in the Yangtse River. Now, in 1933, partly perhaps to resume their aerial odysseys, partly to escape from the harrassment of a gluttonous press, they set forth once again.

They were effectively a high-powered two-person team commissioned by Pan American Airways, to whom Charles was still a technical consultant. The objective was to survey conditions across the North Atlantic, and probably the South Atlantic too, and report back on the operational aspects, the commercial prospects, and even the political nuances that would be faced when launching a trans-Atlantic air service. Juan Trippe, the visionary head of Pan Am, had encountered a certain lack of enthusiasm in his approach to the British, who were understandably reluctant to offer full traffic rights until they were ready to reciprocate with services of their own; and they did not have the aircraft.

Trippe Hedges His Bets

The Lindberghs could possibly have been directed to explore an alternative route to Europe, one that could by-pass Britain, if absolutely necessary. At all events, there was a strong Scandinavian emphasis during the initial, eastbound stages of the epic journey, quite apart from Charles's wish to visit the land of his ancestors, Sweden. The first important destination

Anne Lindbergh had won her aeronautical spurs during the flight to the Orient in 1931 (see pages 40–42), becoming an accomplished radio operator and navigator. These were in the days before voice radio, and her proficiency in both sending and receiving high-speed morse code astonished many a professional.

was Copenhagen, Denmark. The ports of call, after leaving Newfoundland/Labrador (then a British colony) were in Greenland, Iceland, and the Faeroe Islands—all Danish territories at that time. And the supply and depot ship, the *Jelling*, was chartered from the Danish Maersk shipping line.

The Lockheed Sirius at Angmassalik, Greenland, on the Jelling *Expedition. The boy on the wing may have been the one that christened the aircraft* Tingmissartoq *('The One That Flies Like a Big Bird'). (National Air and Space Museum)*

Thus, if Britain (or France, which tended to take the same view as Britain) wished to procrastinate, then Trippe could, with Danish cooperation, establish a trans-Atlantic route by the northern perimeter. No doubt the Lindberghs reported on the hazards that might be encountered in those Arctic regions, especially during the winter.

The Jelling

Ships have often played a part in early airline trans-oceanic pioneering. The French used fast destroyers to link the two ends of the early Aéropostale route across the South Atlantic, during the early 1930s. The Germans used ocean liners and specially built depot ships to catapult mailplanes over the South and the North Atlantic. And Pan American itself established its trans-Pacific route with the essential support of the depot ship, the *North Haven*. Now, to act as a supply ship, and also to act as a refuge for tired aviators during their sojourn in the frozen north, the Maersk Line *Jelling* made its own inestimable contribution, at least as far as Iceland (see page 46).

European Air Tour

The Lindberghs spent close to three months in Europe, after arriving at Copenhagen on 26 August. They took two weeks vacation in Sweden, before going to Moscow, via Finland. They then proceeded to the British Isles, via Norway, visiting a possible flying boat base site in Ireland, and inspecting the English base at Southampton. Early in November, they made their way to Lisbon, thence to the Azores, where they no doubt considered the implications of the 'Horta Swell.' Deciding not to chance a nonstop flight to Newfoundland, they went south to the Canary Islands, where Anne Lindbergh established a new long-distance record for wireless communication by making contact with Long Island, New York, 3,000 miles away.

Home Again

Crossing the South Atlantic to Brazil, Anne kept in touch with some Pan American radio stations and also with the German depot ship *Westfalen*, stationed halfway across. They took a side trip up the Amazon River to Manaus, before retracing some of the route that they had flown eight years previously along the West Indian airline chain. They arrived back in New York on 19 December 1933, just in time for Christmas. Sadly, a combination of circumstances was to result in their staying in the United States for almost exactly only two years; and then they were off again to Europe, this time with a far different agenda.

. . . and Atlantic Epic, 1933

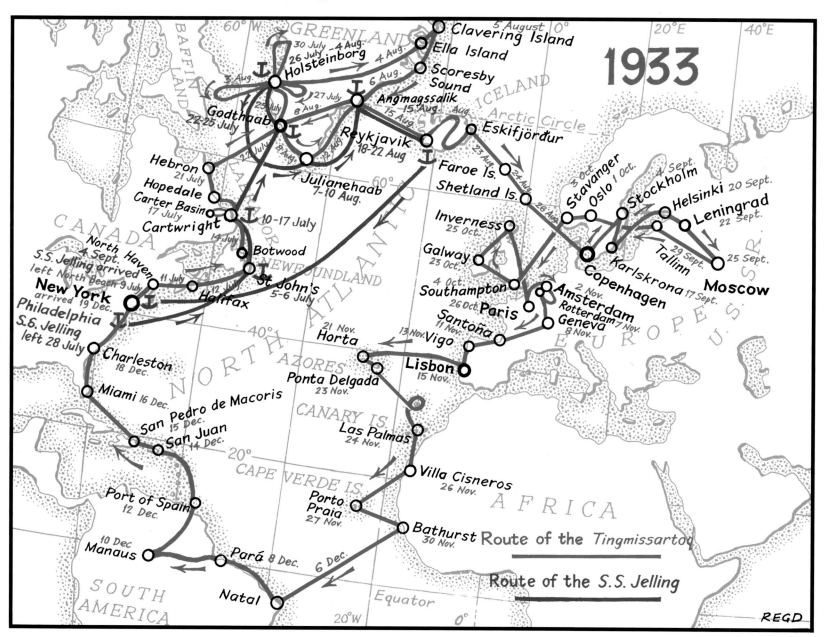

1933

Route of the *Tingmissartoq*

Route of the *S.S. Jelling*

Clavering Island 5 August
Ella Island
Scoresby Sound
Angmagssalik 15 Aug.
Eskifjördur
Reykjavik 18-22 Aug.
Holsteinborg 30 July - 4 Aug. / 26 July / 3 Aug. / 4 Aug. / 6 Aug.
Godthaab 22-25 July / 25 July / 27 July / 8 Aug.
Julianehaab 7-10 Aug.
Faroe Is.
Shetland Is.
Stavanger 3 Oct.
Oslo 1 Oct.
Stockholm 4 Sept.
Helsinki 20 Sept.
Leningrad 22 Sept.
Tallinn 29 Sept.
Karlskrona
Moscow 25 Sept. / 17 Sept.
Copenhagen
Inverness 25 Oct.
Galway 23 Oct.
Amsterdam 2 Nov.
Rotterdam 7 Nov.
Paris 26 Oct.
Geneva 8 Nov.
Southampton 4 Oct.
Santoña 11 Nov.
Vigo 13 Nov.
Horta 21 Nov.
Ponta Delgada 23 Nov.
Lisbon 15 Nov.
Las Palmas 24 Nov.
Villa Cisneros 26 Nov.
Porto Praia 27 Nov.
Bathurst 30 Nov.

Hebron 21 July
Hopedale
Carter Basin 17 July
Cartwright 10-17 July / 14 July
Botwood 11 July
St. John's 5-6 July
North Haven 4 Sept.
S.S. Jelling arrived left North Beach 9 July
New York arrived 19 Dec.
Philadelphia S.S. Jelling left 28 July
Halifax 12 July
Charleston 18 Dec.
Miami 16 Dec.
San Pedro de Macoris 15 Dec.
San Juan 14 Dec.
Port of Spain 12 Dec.
Manaus 10 Dec.
Pará 8 Dec.
Natal 6 Dec.

CANADA
BAFFIN LAND
GREENLAND
ICELAND
Arctic Circle
NEWFOUNDLAND
NORTH ATLANTIC
AZORES
CANARY IS.
CAPE VERDE IS.
AFRICA
EUROPE
U.S.S.R.
SOUTH AMERICA
Equator

60°W / 60°N / 40°N / 20°N / 0° / 20°E / 40°E / 20°W / 20°

REGD

45

The *Jelling*

Sea and Air Partnerships

Paradoxically, while the passenger- and mail-carrying shipping lines were the first to be usurped by the transport airplanes, ships were often to be useful partners rather than rivals. In 1919, the U.S. Navy provided an almost end-to-end procession of vessels to support the first Atlantic crossing by the NC-4. In 1924, the Douglas World Cruisers were assisted by depot ships in their round-the-world epic flight. During the 1930s, the French and the German air routes to South America across the South Atlantic both depended on ships. In the case of Aéropostale, fast destroyers made the connection between aircraft flying from Europe to and from West Africa, and aircraft in Brazil to and from Natal. Deutsche Luft Hansa's Dornier Wal flying boats used specially-designed depot ships to act like mid-ocean aircraft carriers. In 1935, the *North Haven* supply ship provided the men and materials to build the flying boat bases for Pan American's trans-Pacific route. The *Jelling* was in honorable company.

The picture below, at the harbor at Godthaab, in Greenland, evokes the solitude and tranquillity of that remote land. The Tingmissartoq *is dwarfed by even a small two-masted fishing vessel. The S.S. Jelling (right), depot ship for the aircraft, and haven of rest for the tired pilots, lies at anchor. The portside building was one of the largest structures along the entire 1,500-mile west coast of Greenland.*

A Great Team

Charles Lindbergh relaxes at Hebron, Labrador, towards the end of July 1933. The summer in Labrador seems to have been quite mild, but rolled-up sleeves were not to be the dress code for very long.

During their flight around Greenland, Charles and Anne stopped on 4 August at the camp of the Danish geologist and explorer, Lauge Koch. The camp was at Ella Island, at a latitude of about 74° N, just south of the Lindbergh's most northerly port of call. Koch was there to compile the first accurate map of the convoluted coastline of north-eastern Greenland.

On their way to Moscow, the Lindberghs called at Helsinki. They were always grateful for being able to come ashore without running the gauntlet of press photographers. (Courtesy John Wegg)

Even though the Sirius flight across the Atlantic was made during the summer months, scenes such as this, with giant icebergs making their way towards the ocean, were not uncommon. No doubt, Charles put in a detailed report to Pan American Airways.

The arrival at Copenhagen (after calling at Greenland, Iceland, and the Faroe Islands, all of which at that time were Danish territories) was a minor triumph. They were greeted by the Danish Royal Navy and by some enthusiastic onlookers.

Charles and Anne stopped for a day in the Shetland Islands, for a little relaxation. But Charles was always on the move (while Anne wrote her diary). He is seen here, chatting to some local folk. The aircraft is a de Havilland D.H.84 Dragon, used experimentally by the Scottish Motor Traction (S.M.T.) Company. (Courtesy Hugh Cowin)

Into the Wilderness

Escape to Serenity

In a mental state of despair and aggravation, the Lindberghs decided to escape from the spotlight and on 21 December 1935 boarded a ship, in strict secrecy, and sailed for England. No one could blame them. Their second son, Jon, had been born on 16 August 1932; yet the blare of publicity and press intimidation was such that they had to live and move only with an armed guard.

In England they found peace and tranquillity. They made friends, had a country home in Kent, and were able to live a normal life; or at least a life that suited a unique aviation partnership such as theirs. Also there was a family to bring up. On 12 May 1937, another son, Land, was born; and they adopted the English love of dogs, who became part of the family. They bought a private aircraft, a Miles Mohawk, and proceeded to use it in much the same way that ordinary folk would use a motor car.

Flirtation with the Third Reich

In July 1936 the Lindberghs visited Germany and met many people in high places, including distinguished aviators, such as Hans von Gronau, veteran trans-Atlantic flyer, and Air Marshal Hermann Goering, veteran flyer of the Great War of 1914–1918. As an aviator himself, Charles seemed to have been much impressed by all that he saw, and the driving sentiment of German expansionist policies and propaganda seemed not to have given him much concern. He was also inclined to overlook the obvious discrimination against the Jews, and the tendency to glorify the Teutonic race.

Charles and Anne flew their Mohawk back to Germany three times during the next two years, culminating in a tour in 1938, in which he observed the demonstrated strength of the Luftwaffe, and became convinced that Germany was all-powerful; and further, that German dominance would not be a bad thing for Europe as a whole. On 18 October, he was taken by surprise at a reception, when Goering pinned a medal on his chest. He could hardly have refused it at the time; but regrettably, much later, he did not disclaim it. Such was his impression of Germany that he even considered the idea of taking up residence in Berlin.

While there was much evidence to support his judgement of the Luftwaffe's growing strength, his outspoken remarks offended many in Britain—the country that had given him solace when he needed it—and France, for whom he seemed to have little respect. Once, in Paris, he even suggested to the French that they should buy a fleet of bombers from Germany.

In June 1938, the Lindberghs were given a home on the little island of Illiec, in Brittany; and on 8 April 1939, with the clouds of war thickened, they returned to the U.S.A., convinced that England and France were finished as great nations.

America First

Almost immediately upon his return, General Arnold, Chief of the Army Air Corps, assigned a Curtiss-Wright P-36A pursuit aircraft to Charles for his exclusive use. Totally involved with all things to do with aviation, he was on hand on 2 May 1939 to welcome Vladimir Kokkinaki, the Soviet pilot who had flown from Moscow, had force-landed in New Brunswick, but had arrived in New York with greetings to the President.

Lindbergh did not see eye to eye with President Roosevelt. Back in 1934, he had strongly opposed the cancellation of the air mail contracts. Now, possibly offering an olive branch (or perhaps hoping to head off more opposition from an influential direction) FDR offered Charles the chairmanship of the Civil Aeronautics Authority, a position that he could have handled well. But he refused, and instead began to support isolationist groups which opposed America's involvement in a European war.

The vehemence of his support, particularly of the movement known as America First, polarized public and political opinion, not least because he was such a prominent figure, and, only a few years previously, a great hero. T.W.A., the airline that had, since 1930, proclaimed itself as The Lindbergh Line, dropped the idea on 5 December 1939. For his part, Charles conducted an almost personal feud with the President, opposing his policy of helping Britain and France to combat the conquest of Europe by Nazi Germany, and testifying against the Lend-Lease Bill on 23 January 1941.

Things came to a head when, after a series of speeches in support of the America First organization, he declared, in Des Moines, on 11 September 1941 (and reiterated the sentiments two weeks later) that the war in Europe was the fault of Britain, France, and the Jews. Somehow or other, he seemed to think that a German-ruled Europe, even with Adolf Hitler as its ruler, would be good for America as well.

Three months later, Charles Lindbergh's views were irrelevant; for on 7 December, Japan destroyed much of the U.S. Pacific fleet in a surprise attack at Pearl Harbor, Honolulu, and, like it or not, the United States was at war with the Axis powers, including the Germany which Lindbergh had respected so much.

Charles Lindbergh was able to interest himself in many things, not necessarily directly connected with his own flying. In September 1935, he visited Roswell, New Mexico, to meet Dr. R.H. Goddard (center), the distinguished rocket scientist, in front of the experimental launch tower. On Goddard's right is Harry F. Guggenheim, Charles's former benefactor and friend.

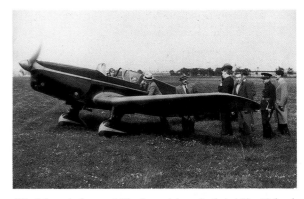

This informal picture of Charles and Anne in their Miles Mohawk, taken in the late 1930s, reflects the comparatively relaxed environment in which they were able to escape the glare of publicity that they had left behind, following the sensationalism of the kidnapping episode.

Private 'Plane

Miles M.12 Mohawk

Length/Span: .....25/35 feet
Engine .....Menasco Buccaneer
(200 hp)
Seating ....2 incl. pilot
Cruise Speed ....170 mph
MGTOW ....2,620 lb
Normal Range ...1,400 st. miles

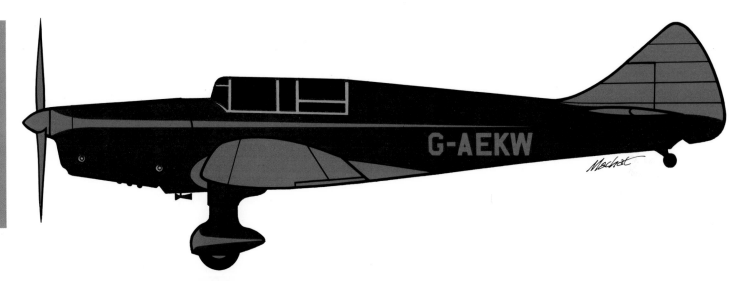

G-AEKW

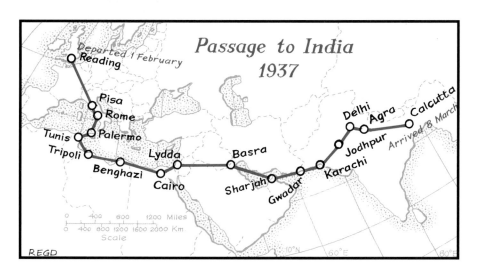

Passage to India 1937

Departed 1 February

Reading
Pisa
Rome
Palermo
Tunis
Tripoli
Benghazi
Cairo
Lydda
Basra
Sharjah
Gwadar
Karachi
Jodhpur
Delhi
Agra
Calcutta
Arrived 8 March

400 800 1200 Miles
400 800 1200 1600 2000 Km.
Scale

10°N   60°E   80°E

REGD

Mission to Moscow 1938

0 100 200 300 400 500 Miles
0 200 400 600 800 Km
Scale

Reading
Lympne
St Inglevert
Morlaix
Paris
Stuttgart
Hanover
Warsaw
Prague
Olmutz
Krakov
Cluj
Odessa
Kiev
Kharkov
Rostov
Mogilev
Moscow

20 Sept.
10 Sept.
8 Sept.
16 Aug.
17 Aug.
26 Aug.
28 Aug.
30 Aug.
31 Aug.
1 Sept.
2 Sept.

REGD

Rehabilitation

Reassessment

Charles Lindbergh's streak of obstinacy must have been severely tested by this time; for in the fall of 1940 the Luftwaffe, which he had declared to be omnipotent, had failed, with apparently far superior air strength, to win the Battle of Britain. He had maintained that the British aircraft were inferior; alternatively that the British as a whole lacked courage. He had even used the word 'decadent.' During the war years, he was obliged to keep his more extreme views to himself, but on no occasion did he admit that he had been, to put it mildly, disingenuous.

The Family Man

Just as Charles's flying career is identified mainly with the famous New York-Paris flight of 1927, so is his role as a husband and father identified mainly with the tragedy of Charles Junior in 1932. Yet he was deeply concerned with his family, regarding Anne as a true kindred spirit as well as a wife, and genuinely proud of her accomplishments as a writer, co-pilot, and radio-operator/navigator; and above all as a good mother to their five children: Jon (born in 1932), Land (1937), Ann Spencer (1940), Scott (1942), and Reeve (1945). As a father, he encouraged independence and fortitude—remembering perhaps his own stamina-testing childhood—but at the same time advised common-sense precautions against the possibility of error. He tried to pass on to his children the same qualities that had enabled him to beat all the odds in 1927, and to remind them that good luck did not come by accident.

The Perfusion Pump

One disappointment must have been his estrangement from Dr. Alexis Carrel, a French Nobel Laureate with whom he had worked at the Rockefeller Institute in 1934, when Anne's elder sister became terminally ill. Carrel described the principle of an apparatus that could keep organs alive outside the body, while operations took place; and Charles drew upon his mechanical skills to invent, during four years of experiment, the perfusion pump. This was recognized as a definite contribution to medical knowledge and he was to share with Carrel the credit for the publication of *The Culture of Organs*.

Unhappily, in 1940, Dr. Carrel telephoned him, asking that, in one of his radio addresses, he would make a friendly reference to France, to encourage the French resistance to Nazi conquest. Lindbergh refused. Carrel disliked the Germans (and what true Frenchman would not, at that time?),

whereas Lindbergh still thought they should be the salvation of Europe against the Bolsheviks.

The unkindest cut of all was that Carrel, who went back to France, died in 1944, having been accused of collaboration with the Germans.

Ford to the Rescue

On 20 December 1941, Charles Lindbergh wrote to General Hap Arnold, offering his services to the Army Air Corps. Receiving no reply, he telephoned Arnold on 10 January 1942, but was passed on to the Secretary of War, Henry L. Stimson. But the latter's colleagues in the Administration, notably Secretary of the Interior, Harold Ickes, were not kindly disposed to welcoming back to the fold a man who had so passionately railed against the President and all he stood for. And on 13 January, Stimson courteously but firmly turned him down. Even his old friend, Juan Trippe, was unable to help. Lindbergh had outplayed his hand.

Then, on 21 March, came salvation, and something of a balm to hurt pride. Henry Ford asked Charles to visit him. Ford was going into mass-production of bombers for the Army Air Force, and he recognized in Lindbergh the qualities and talents that he needed to guide him into this unknown territory of technology.

On 3 April, Charles Lindbergh became a technical consultant to the Ford organization, attached to the enormous Willow Run plant, still under construction in Detroit. He held that position until the fall of 1943.

Quality Controller

Charles was in a somewhat privileged position at the Ford plant, having been invited by the great Henry Ford himself. But he was careful not to interfere too obtrusively with the Ford hierarchy that was charged with the task of producing large bomber aircraft using production methods not far removed from that of building motor cars.

He was highly critical at first, as the huge Willow Run plant began to take shape and B-24 sub-assemblies arrived

from San Diego, and the work force came to terms with more refined specifications, finer tolerances, new metals, new inventions and innovations. The production line was almost a mile long, and employed up to 100,000 workers at its peak. His early criticism was justified, as the first completed aircraft off the line were not acceptable by his standards. He was able to advise at the highest level, and because of his hands-on experience and track record as a supreme pilot who had also tested and analysed airplane performance, his views were respected.

Ford's mass production methods bore fruit. By Spring 1944, 400 B-24 Liberator bombers came off the production line in one month.

These two Corsairs, pictured on patrol in the western Pacific, illustrate the unusual 'inverted gull' wing shape. These were hinged, so that they could be folded upwards and inwards, thus conserving space in the hangars and on the decks of aircraft carriers. (Courtesy: David Ostrowski Collection)

This picture of the versatile Vought F4U-1D Corsair clearly shows its bomb-carrying capability. (Courtesy: David Ostrowski Collection)

(Left) In an impressive mass-production effort, the Ford Willow Run plant turned out nearly 7,000 Consolidated B-24 Liberator bombers. (Courtesy: David Ostrowski Collection)

Rendezvous in Rabaul

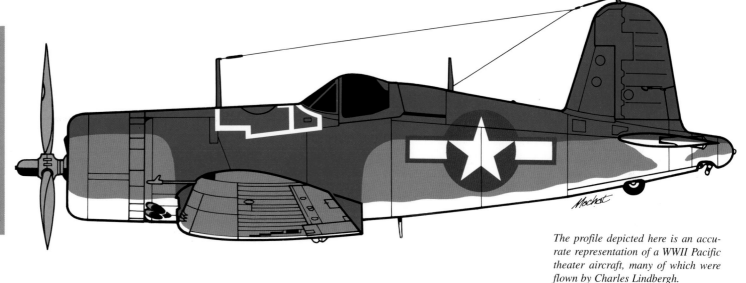

Vought F4U-1D Corsair

Length/Span:	.33/41 feet
Engine	Pratt & Whitney R-2800 (2,000 hp)
Seating	1 pilot
Cruise Speed	180 mph
MGTOW	14,000 lb
Normal Range	1,000 st. miles

The profile depicted here is an accurate representation of a WWII Pacific theater aircraft, many of which were flown by Charles Lindbergh.

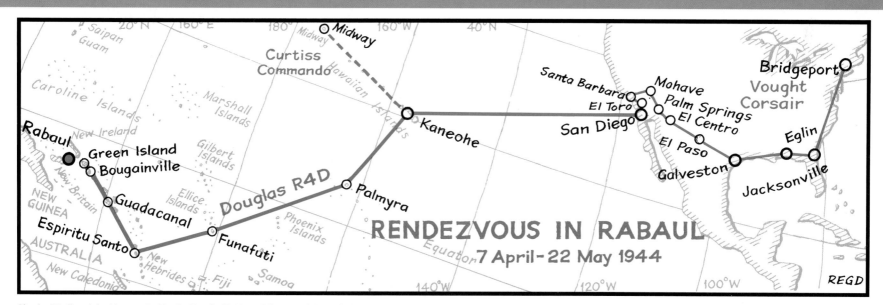

RENDEZVOUS IN RABAUL
7 April - 22 May 1944

Charles Lindbergh had been asked by the Vought division of the United Aircraft Corporation to examine critically the performance capability of the Vought Corsair naval attack aircraft. He obtained some operational experience by flying one from the Bridgeport plant to San Diego. He then took a Douglas R4D (naval DC-3) across the Pacific, so as to participate in the Corsair's front-line operations.

War Duty

Scenic Route to Rabaul (and other Beach Resorts)

In April 1944, Charles was given the opportunity to serve overseas. As a representative of the United Aircraft Corporation, he was attached to the U.S. Navy to test the Vought F4U Corsair fighter aircraft in the front line, specifically to Rabaul, on the island of New Britain. This was no sinecure. Defining the terms of his assignment as attaching himself to the Marines, he made several dangerous patrol missions to Rabaul and Kavieng in May and June. He then moved to Hollandia, New Guinea, with the 475th Fighter Group, and continued his evaluations by flying combat missions with P-38 Lightnings, from the end of June until 17 August, when he was recalled by the authorities, which had become apprehensive as to the consequences of the famous Lone Eagle falling into Japanese hands.

He left Brisbane on 25 August, in a Naval Air Transport Service (NATS) Consolidated PB2Y-3R Coronado (flown by Pan American crews), and more or less hitched rides back across the Pacific on Navy aircraft to Oakland, and then by United Air Lines and T.W.A. back home.

Charles Lindbergh had added some more colorful episodes to his already unmatched flying career. He was credited with one 'kill,' and on two occasions came within a hair's breadth of being killed himself. He came face to face with contradictions and complexities of moral issues, as he was confronted with the appalling loss of life, the harsh acts of cruelty, and the often gruesome sequels. He was appalled by the atrocities committed on both sides, and the sheer lack of humanity displayed.

Contribution to the War Effort

He did his job. In the case of the Corsair, he recommended that it could carry a 2,000 lb bomb (instead of the standard 1,000 lb); and was able to prove that the P-38, properly nursed along when cruising, could have an operating range of 750 miles instead of the 570 hitherto assumed. Both recommendations were well received by the High Command and put into effect. General George Kenney even went so far as to suggest that the P-38's additional range helped to shorten the war and saved thousands of American lives.

Charles Lindbergh had, in the eyes of most Americans, redeemed himself. Even so, he never renounced his previously-held strong opinion that the United States should never have become involved in another world war. And henceforth he kept the more extreme of his political views to himself.

Charles Lindbergh preparing to launch on a P-38 mission at Biak Island, New Guinea in 1944. (Courtesy: David Ostrowski Collection)

Charles Lindbergh served his country well during the Second World War. Here he is acquainting himself with the merits of a carbine.

During the few months that Charles Lindbergh managed to become part of the United States war effort in the southwest Pacific, he never experienced a dull moment. Almost every day, as this map shows, he was on active duty until the time came for him to be recalled, for fear that he might fall into enemy hands.

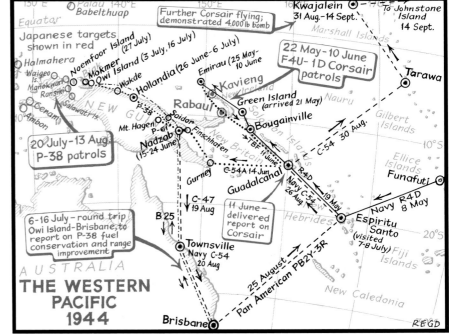

THE WESTERN PACIFIC 1944

Stretching the Envelope

The profile depicted here is an accurate representation of a WW II Pacific theater aircraft, many of which were flown by Charles Lindbergh.

Lockheed P-38L Lightning

Length/Span: . . . . .38/52 feet
Engine . . . .2 x Allison V-1710 (1,475 hp, with 1,600 hp in emergency)

Seating . . . . .1 pilot
MGTOW . . . . .21,600 lb

Cruise speed . . . . .290 mph
Normal Range . . . . .450 st. miles
Maximum Range (with drop tanks) . .2,600 st. miles

20 Years of Piston-engined Progress

During the span of only two decades, aviation technology had advanced spectacularly. From the 'stick-and-string' 70-mph Jenny of 1923, and the 100-mph Ryan of 1927, America entered the Second World War with aircraft that were almost 300 miles an hour faster.

(Courtesy David Ostrowski Collection)

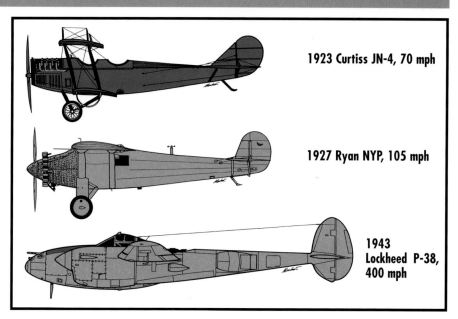

1923 Curtiss JN-4, 70 mph

1927 Ryan NYP, 105 mph

1943 Lockheed P-38, 400 mph

The Autumn Years

Winding Down

For Charles Lindbergh, who had reached the heights of fame, and who had been involved, at the highest level, in both the intellectual and physical aspects of technical progress for almost half a century, slowing down with advancing years was not a transition that he welcomed. This was a man who did not relish the trimmings of polite society. He never danced, and once excused himself from such a function at Buckingham Palace, and sat out a dance with the Queen of England. He was interested in everything; and interest, to him, meant involvement. Thus, progressing from country boyhood in Minnesota, he had driven many kinds of wheeled vehicles, flown every kind of aircraft, had invented an apparatus used in medical science, meddled in politics, written several books (which he claimed earned him more than aviation did), and during the postwar years of middle age, became a conservationist.

Back to Pan American

As soon as practically possible, Juan Trippe, his old friend from the pioneering days in the Caribbean in 1928, took him under the Pan Am wing as a director and consultant. This could have been a polite sinecure, but this was not Charles's nature. He really did advise, and his wisdom, experience, and knowledge in aviation matters were widely respected.

He did not support the idea of a supersonic airliner, even though, during the latter Sixties, the whole world of commercial air transport looked upon such aircraft as the Concorde and the Tupolev Tu-144 as the next generation to follow the Boeing 707s and the DC-8s. He correctly defined the supersonic role as an inefficient use of resources (possibly recalling his work with the P-38 in 1944), and was appalled at the Concorde's thirst for fuel. He was right, when almost all the other so-called experts were wrong. The Concorde burns a ton of fuel for every seat it carries across the Atlantic.

On the other hand, he worked closely with such pragmatic realists as John Borger, Chief Engineer of Pan Am, in studying the development potential of all new airliner projects. Willis Player, head of Pan Am's Public Relations, asserted that "if you are riding on a 747 . . . . . . you are riding in an airplane that Charles Lindbergh helped to bring into being." The 747 has been the airline world's flagship for more than a quarter of a century, and more than 1,000 have come off the production line.

The Press

He and Anne had endured, after his great triumph of 1927, the attention of a ravenous press that deprived him of any privacy, and the hero-worship became an embarrassment. Already intolerant because of this, the newspaper reporters' vulture-like descent on the Lindberghs when their first child was killed in 1932 stretched this tolerance to breaking point. He refused interviews, and abhorred photographers, even to the extent that he often carried a hat, not to wear, but to cover his face when a camera came into view.

Just before the Second World War, after his well-publicized courtship with Germany, he felt that this relationship had been falsely reported—but this time he had himself to blame, partly because of a certain obstinancy and reluctance to modify his extreme views.

Much later, after an unfortunate experience with a postwar BBC (of all organizations!) documentary that he thought was biased, he told John Grierson "My experience has been that the Press, and this pretty much includes television and radio, confuses and cheapens everything it touches."

Few would disagree with this perhaps over-generalized statement, and there are many current examples to support his attitude which came near to being a phobia. On the other hand, he himself never made any concessions; and his experience while living in England during the latter Thirties, when he was left alone, should have encouraged a change of attitude, if not a change of heart.

He was the victim of his own fame. No man achieved greater fame, and no man paid a higher price for that fame.

The Conservationist

As he grew older, Charles Lindbergh became interested in the preservation of wild life. This ranged from the fish in Puget Sound to the American bald eagle and rare birds such as the Philippine monkey-eating eagle. If he lived today, he would undoubtedly be a prominent executive (if not the chairman) of the World Wildlife Fund, and leading the crusade to preserve all the world's endangered species. He even offered to break his own rigid rules of conduct and go on television, if that would guarantee the survival of the blue whale.

He was quoted as declaring "I do not think there is anything more important than conservation, with the exception of human survival, and the two are so closely interlaced that it is hard to separate one from the other."

Charles would occasionally visit the Spirit *at the Smithsonian in Washington, D.C. In 1976, it was transferred to the National Air and Space Museum. (photo: Sam Smith)*

Still a world-wide traveller in his later years, Charles visited Brazil in the late 1960s. He is seen here with Sadia's Dr. Omar Fontana, inspecting the latter's Handley Page Dart Herald. (Courtesy: Omar Fontana)

Last Flight

Humanity Too

If Charles Lindbergh was intensively interested in the conservation of animal life, he was no less concerned with the human race. Aside from being a leading member of the World Wild Life's Survival Service Commission, he was also a director of Panamin—the Private Association for National Minorities. During his wide-spread travels during the 1960s, he became especially interested in the threatened minority tribes in the Philippines, and worked hard with local authorities to preserve their life-styles and customs. He was especially associated with the Tasadays, in Mindanao, the southernmost island of the Philippines, who still lived in the manner of the Stone Age.

During this period, he travelled as an ordinary passenger, eschewing V.I.P. Treatment. He combined his conservation-oriented flying with informal inspection trips for Pan American, and did so with the minimum of fuss, and was always a model traveller.

A Great Flying Life

During his lifetime, Charles Lindbergh flew hundreds of different types of aircraft; and these ranged from the biplanes of the early 1920s to the four-engined bombers of the Second World War. He flew privately and on assignment for great airlines and contributed in no small part to their route planning and operational disciplines.

Many a pilot would have been satisfied with even one of the many great flights that are described in this book. But Charles Lindbergh made a collection of great flights, and in so doing made a priceless contribution to the advancement of aeronautics.

Charles must have spent half of his waking hours flying airplanes. He was arguably the greatest pilot of all time.

Nearing the End

Towards the end of his life, and still seeking seclusion, if not solitude, Charles and Anne purchased a piece of land from his good friend and fellow Pan American executive, Sam Pryor. This was on the island of Maui, and there, far from the Madding Crowd, he built his last home. When, in 1972, he learned that he was dying of blood cancer, he discharged himself from the New York hospital, against the advice of his doctors, and made haste to Maui, where he felt that he would be out of range of batteries of television cameras and sensation-seeking reporters.

The child, it is said, is the Father of the Man. This portrait of Charles in the autumn years of his life recalls his childhood days in the backwoods of the upper Mississippi at Little Falls, Minnesota, where he had hardened himself for a life-long stamina-demanding career.

Death with Dignity

Just for once, he was not in control of his ultimate fate. But even then he influenced the manner of his passing. Anne suggested a suitable hymn for the funeral service. The music was by Bach, but Charles thought the words to be too banal. They ended up with a missionary hymn, sung in Hawaiian.

He arranged every detail of the funeral service, specified the design of the simple coffin, and supervised the digging and construction of the grave. For the gravestone, he chose for its inscription an extract from the 139th psalm, that begins ***"If I take the wings of the morning, and dwell in the uttermost parts of the seas . . ."***

Bibliography

(Author's Note: Close to a hundred books have been written by or about the Lindberghs. This selection lists those that I have used as my main references. These comprise the ones that concentrate on an account of flights and achievements, and I have emphasized in bold type those that have been the most useful for my purpose here. Many other books have addressed the controversial aspects of Charles Lindbergh's political views. For those who wish to delve more deeply into the study of a complex man, a complete listing of relevant publications is to be found in the excellent compendium ***Charles A. Lindbergh: A Bio-Biography,*** by Perry D. Luckett, published by the Greenwood Press, Westport, Connecticut, in 1986.)

Beamish, Richard J. *The Story of Lindbergh, the Lone Eagle.* Philadelphia, The John C. Winston Company, 1927

Crouch, Tom D. (Editor) *Charles A. Lindbergh: An American Life.* Washington, National Air and Space Museum, 1977

Davis, Kenneth S. **The Hero.** New York, Doubleday, 1959

Grierson, John. *I Remember Lindbergh.* New York, Harcourt Brace Jovanovich, 1977

Haines, Lynn and Dora B. *The Lindberghs.* New York, The Vanguard Press, 1931

Keyhoe, Donald E. *Flying with Lindbergh.* New York, G.P. Putnam's Sons, 1928

Lindbergh, Anne M, **North to the Orient.** New York, Harcourt Brace, 1935

_____. ***Bring Me a Unicorn*** (Diaries, 1922–28). New York, Harcourt Brace Jovanovich, 1972

_____. ***Hour of Gold, Hour of Lead*** (Diaries, 1929–32). New York, Harcourt Brace Jovanovich, 1973

_____. ***Locked Rooms and Open Doors*** (Diaries, 1933–35). New York, Harcourt Brace Jovanovich, 1974

_____. ***The Flower and the Nettle*** (Diaries, 1936–39) Harcourt Brace Jovanovich, 1976

Lindbergh, Charles A. ***"We"*** New York, G.P. Putnam's Sons, 1927

_____. *Of Flight and Life.* New York, Charles Scribner's Sons, 1948

_____. ***The Spirit of St. Louis.*** New York, Charles Scribner's Sons, 1953

_____. ***The Wartime Journals of Charles A. Lindbergh.*** New York, Harcourt Brace Javanovich, 1970

_____. *An Autobiography of Values.* New York, Jovanovich,1974

Milton, Joyce. *Loss of Eden.* New York, Harper Collins, 1993

Mosley, Leonard. **Lindbergh—A Biography.** New York, Doubleday, 1976

Ross, Walter S. *The Last Hero.* New York, Harper & Row, 1964

Index